D0372397

# Do you remember Technology

## GEEKS, GADGETS + GIZMOS

BY
MICHAEL GITTER,
SYLVIE ANAPOL,
AND ERIKA GLAZER

**CHRONICLE BOOKS**
SAN FRANCISCO

**DESIGN & ART DIRECTION:**
Red Herring Design: Carol Bobolts, Deb Schuler, Robin Rosenthal, supermodel Adam Chiu, Susan Baldaserini

**PHOTO RESEARCH:**
Marie Walker, Tish King

**RESEARCH ASSISTANTS:**
Bay Anapol, Elizabeth Fasolino

**PHOTOGRAPHY AND ILLUSTRATIONS:**
Courtesy Apple Computer, Inc., Archive Photos, © 1976 The Book Publishing Company, Courtesy British Airways, Classic PIO Library, © 1979 Columbia Pictures Industries, Inc., Corbis/Bettmann-UPI, The Everett Collection, © 1969 Fawcett Publications, Inc., Courtesy Federal Express, Rube Goldberg, Inc., © 1999 Harold & Esther Edgerton Foundation, courtesy of Palm Press, Inc., Courtesy IBM, Liason International/ © Werner Krutein, © 1999 Magic Eye, Inc., Courtesy Maxell Corporation of America, Courtesy Motorola, Movie Star News, PhotoDisc, Inc., Joanne Savio, © 1999 Robert Silvers/Runaway Technology, Courtesy Smithsonian National Museum of American History, Courtesy Texas Instruments, Courtesy Thomson Consumer Electronics, © 1983 Time, Inc. Reprinted by Permission, © Tony Stone Images/Martin Barraud, © 1986 Tri-Star Pictures, Inc., © 1982 Walt Disney Productions, © Warner Bros.

**MANY THANKS TO:**
We'd like to thank the many people who've assisted and inspired us, both directly and indirectly, in creating *Do You Remember Technology?*, our third book in the series. **Our associates, participants in our brainstorming sessions, and other friends:** Karen Berry, Debra Calman, Alex Channing, Kim Cohen, Thom Dean, John Dyche, Wayne Edelman, Andrew Frank, Jane Goetz, Valeria Lempert, Peter Levy, Richard Metzger, Michael Mueller, Eric Newill, Marc "we got the spelling right this time" Pascucci, Michelle Raadschelders, and the staff at Raincoast Books, Carla Ruben, Erica Ruben, Michael Rucker, James Salkind, David Sarner, Billy Stern, Judy Taylor, Bonnie Topfer-Vozar, Beverly Tracy, Alanna Velasquez, Pim Winter. We would also like to thank **everyone who wrote, e-mailed, and faxed in suggestions**, and the technical additions provided by the MIS departments of many companies including m@x RACKS and Chronicle Books. **Our families:** (Sylvie's) Paul Vaccari, Julius Anapol, Chris, Erica, Mariana, and Matthew Vaccari. (Erika's) Alex, Zach, Rosie, Minky, and Joe Hill. (Michael's) Barbara, Richard, Lory, Kelly, David, Cindy, Nicolas, and Luke. **Our friends at Chronicle including:** Sarah Malarkey, Mikyla Bruder, Brenda Tucker, Julia Flagg, Cynthia Wallin, and Chris Hemesath. And most of all to Carol Bobolts, Deb Schuler, and their staff at Red Herring Design, who made this and so many other amazing books of ours — come to life. **Red Herring would like to thank** our families who have cheerfully packed up contents of their basements and shipped them to NY (with the proviso that nothing returns): Dorothy and Richard Bobolts, Sue and Skip Schuler, Mary Ann and Art Knechtel; Lynn Kowalewski; Joanne and Jim Savio; Jim Peacock for quickly responding to frantic e-mails; eBay; and especially Todd Miller and his "Associates" for keeping the boxes up and running.

Printed in Singapore

Library of Congress Cataloging-in-Publication Data available.
ISBN 0-8118-2772-0

Distributed in Canada by
Raincoast Books
8680 Cambie Street
Vancouver, B.C. V6P 6M9

1   2   3   4   5   6   7   8   9   10

Chronicle Books
85 Second Street
San Francisco, CA 94105
www.chroniclebooks.com

TO THE POPEILS :)

3

**I**n our last two *Do You Remember?* editions, we celebrated American pop culture. Now, as humanity crosses over into the next millennium—and technology whirs along faster than a Pentium III chip*—we decided it timely to look back at the triumphs and turkeys of 20th-century technology.

As we waxed nostalgic about a slower and sometimes clunkier time, we uncovered ingenious machines and breakthrough products—some of which are utterly obsolete, some we wish were still around, some that are back in vogue, and others that have simply stood the test of time.

Do you remember . . . Your ears popping as you rolled up the windows of your VW bug? Working out without Spandex? Attempting to cook a real meal in a microwave? Wondering if a piece of SkyLab would land in your backyard? The smell of mimeograph paper? VCRs costing $1,000? A computer that was bigger than you? A vacation when you couldn't be contacted?

We hope your stroll down memory lane is as fascinating as it was for us. Plus, *Do You Remember? Technology* features an index where you can find out the whos, wheres, and whys of these technological wonders. And if the urge hits, send us your suggestions for our next book. You can e-mail us through our Website at www.doyouremember.com or fax us at (212) 873-7223.

*Michael* *Sylvie* and *Erika*

*By the time this book hits your shelf, Pentium X may be the industry standard.

"**Honey, the rabbit died...**"

before Lamaze

metal strollers and high chairs with sharp edges

plastic pants that went over cloth diapers

before EPT

cloth diapers

before the pill

diaper pails

copper coil IUD

fathers-to-be pacing in the waiting room, instead of camcording in the delivery room

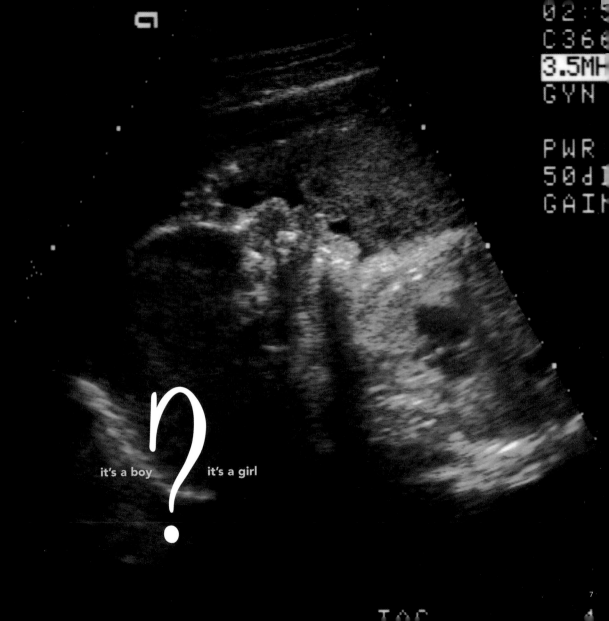

# Baby on board

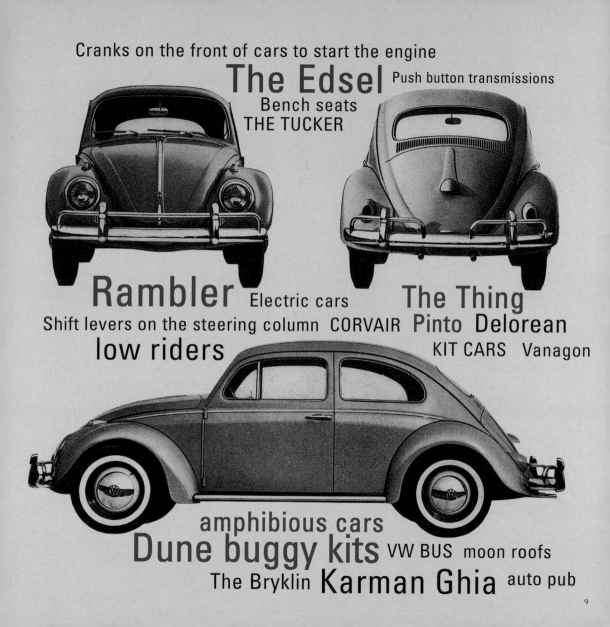

Cranks on the front of cars to start the engine
The Edsel  Push button transmissions
Bench seats
THE TUCKER

Rambler  Electric cars  The Thing
Shift levers on the steering column  CORVAIR  Pinto  Delorean
low riders  KIT CARS  Vanagon

amphibious cars
Dune buggy kits  VW BUS  moon roofs
The Bryklin  Karman Ghia  auto pub

10

motorcycles with sidecars · Harley Panheads · Ramjet Fuel Injection · '78 Engines · Powerglide automatic transmission · safety glass in windshields · Dual exhaust · The Pacer · The Hornet · The Gremlin · Jeep during the AMC years · BSA · Henderson · Norton · The first Japanese import · Honda CB55 · handshifts · Minibikes · Indian motorcycles · Datsun · The Chevette

FOR USE AS A
MOTOR FUEL ONLY

CONTAINS
LEAD

( TETRAETHYL )

D.D.T.
Powerful Insecticide
Harmless to Humans

Applied by

TODD INSECT FOG SPRAYER
Nassau County Extermination Service
L. I. State Park Comm.

*Gulf Space Sprayer*

red dye #2 mercury Love Canal
thalidomide lead paint

creeple **peeple**
**CREEPY** crawlers
**shrinky** dinks
incredible **edibles**
**SUPER ELASTIC** bubble plastic
**ouija** boards

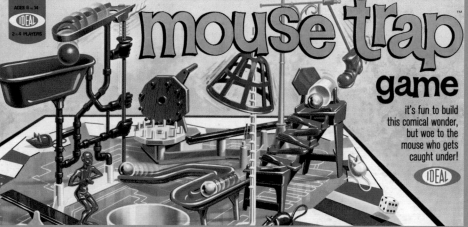

**mouse trap**
game

it's fun to build
this comical wonder,
but woe to the
mouse who gets
caught under!

IDEAL

AGES 6 to 14
IDEAL
2 to 4 PLAYERS

**chemistry** sets
**radio control** planes
**bing** bang **boing**
**super** balls
**magic** rocks
silly **putty**

RUBE GOLDBERG WALKS IN HIS SLEEP, STROLLS THROUGH A CACTUS FIELD IN HIS BARE FEET, AND SCREAMS OUT AN IDEA FOR A SELF-OPERATING NAPKIN. AS YOU RAISE SPOON OF SOUP (A) TO YOUR MOUTH IT PULLS STRING (B), THEREBY JERKING LADLE (C) WHICH THROWS CRACKER (D) PAST PARROT (E). PARROT JUMPS AFTER CRACKER AND PERCH (F) TILTS, UPSETTING SEEDS (G) INTO PAIL (H). EXTRA WEIGHT IN PAIL PULLS CORD (I) WHICH OPENS AND LIGHTS AUTOMATIC CIGAR LIGHTER (J), SETTING OFF SKY-ROCKET (K) WHICH CAUSES SICKLE (L) TO CUT STRING (M) AND ALLOW PENDULUM WITH ATTACHED NAPKIN TO SWING BACK AND FORTH THEREBY WIPING OFF YOUR CHIN. AFTER THE MEAL, SUBSTITUTE A HARMONICA FOR THE NAPKIN AND YOU'LL BE ABLE TO ENTERTAIN THE GUESTS WITH A LITTLE MUSIC.

RUBE GOLDBERG IS THE R AND C OF RUBE GOLDBERG INC.

# "They don't bite – they don't even light"

bug zappers

calamine lotion

ant traps

Shell No-Pest Strips

before Combat

Aeroxa
FLY-CATCHER
WITH THUMB TACK
Exclusive Fly Lure
BEST

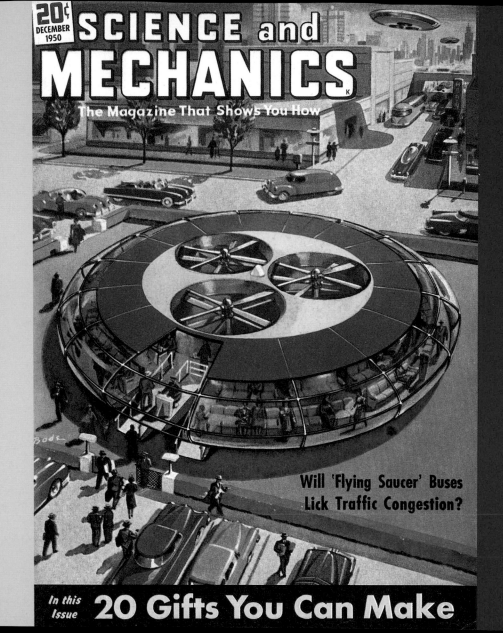

20¢
DECEMBER
1950

# SCIENCE and MECHANICS
### The Magazine That Shows You How

Will 'Flying Saucer' Buses
Lick Traffic Congestion?

*In this Issue*
# 20 Gifts You Can Make

16mb

# WHAM-O FRISBEE ®

AMERICA'S FAVORITE GAME OF CATCH!

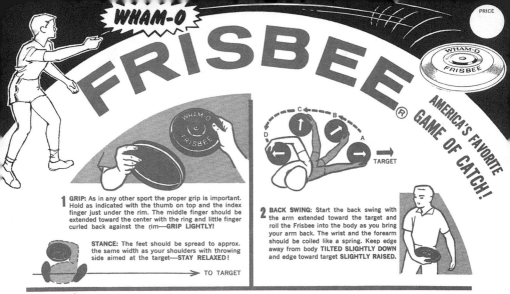

**1 GRIP:** As in any other sport the proper grip is important. Hold as indicated with the thumb on top and the index finger just under the rim. The middle finger should be extended toward the center with the ring and little finger curled back against the rim—**GRIP LIGHTLY!**

**STANCE:** The feet should be spread to approx. the same width as your shoulders with throwing side aimed at the target—**STAY RELAXED!**

TO TARGET

**2 BACK SWING:** Start the back swing with the arm extended toward the target and roll the Frisbee into the body as you bring your arm back. The wrist and the forearm should be coiled like a spring. Keep edge away from body **TILTED SLIGHTLY DOWN** and edge toward target **SLIGHTLY RAISED.**

---

## WHAM-O FRISBEE ® — THROW and CATCH GAME

Enjoyed by top athletes around the world, manufactured by WHAM-O, leaders in new sports ideas. Frisbee is a sport that can be enjoyed by amateurs and pros alike. The more you practice the more you enjoy Frisbee. Demonstrate your ability at beach and park, "it's a ball." Read the following instructions and become an expert.

---

**3 FLAT THROW:** Start throw from shoulder extending arm towards target. Keep wrist coiled until arm is extended then snap wrist in a whipping motion **SPINNING** Frisbee. Throw with your wrist and **FOLLOW THRU.** As you start throw **STEP TOWARD TARGET. IMPORTANT:** Keep Frisbee in same plane during throw. **FORM IS EVERYTHING.**

FRONT VIEW OF POSITION "C"

KEEP TILTED DOWN

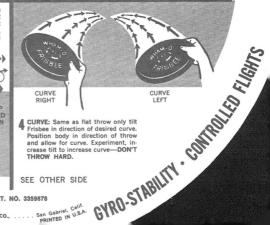

CURVE RIGHT

CURVE LEFT

**4 CURVE:** Same as flat throw only tilt Frisbee in direction of desired curve. Position body in direction of throw and allow for curve. Experiment, increase tilt to increase curve—**DON'T THROW HARD.**

SEE OTHER SIDE

BOOMERANGS · SAILS · FLOATS · SKIPS · GYRO-STABILITY · CONTROLLED FLIGHTS

©1967 WHAM-O MFG. CO., ..... San Gabriel, Calif. PRINTED IN U.S.A.

U.S. PAT. NO. 3359678

STOCK NO. 132

PRICE

FOOD ADDITIVES
AND PRESERVATIVES

BEFORE "INSTANT"

JELL-O 1-2-3

WHEN THERE WERE
4 BASIC FOOD GROUPS

FREEZE DRIED

BEFORE FROZEN FOOD

PB & J IN THE SAME JAR

STOVETOP JIFFY POP

MARSHMALLOW
FLUFF

WHEN WATTAGE WAS THE ONLY CHOICE • SODIUM VAPOR • LOW VOLTAGE

BEFORE HALOGEN • BLACKLIGHT • MERCURY VAPOR • FLUORESCENT

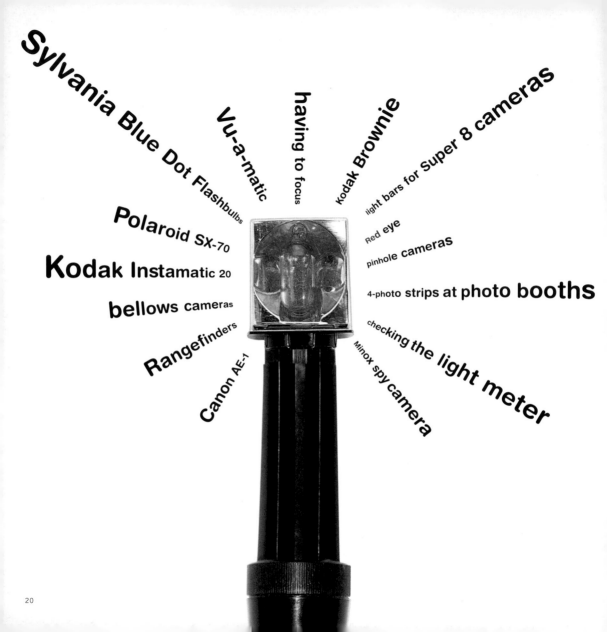

Sylvania Blue Dot Flashbulbs

Vu-a-matic

having to focus

Kodak Brownie

light bars for Super 8 cameras

Red eye

pinhole cameras

4-photo strips at photo booths

checking the light meter

Minox spy camera

Canon AE-1

Rangefinders

bellows cameras

Kodak Instamatic 20

Polaroid SX-70

# THE SWINGER

ultrasuede doubleknit polyester / huckapoo's caprolan kodel nylon rayon dacron orlon banlon antron and soon and soon...

REEL TO REEL TAPE **BATTERY-OPERATED PORTABLE TURNTABLES** 16 RPM **33 1/3 RPM** 45 RPM **78 RPM** Q-SOUND **TRANSISTOR RADIOS** MONO VS STEREO **BEFORE DOLBY** ANALOG **COLORED LIGHTS AND STROBES BLINKING IN TIME TO MUSIC** QUADROPHONIC STEREO

24

$$E=MC^2$$

Drop and cover drills B-52 bomber

Area 51 Neutron bombs

jump jets FLAK Polaris missiles

Armor-piercing bullets

backyard bomb shelters Fallout shelters

The Manhattan Project

Sherman tanks

Drive-in movies ★ Sensurround ★ Technicolor ★ The Cinerama Dome ★ THX ★ Odorama ★ IMAX ★ "Pay no attention to the man behind the screen..." ★ Stop-motion animation ★ Panavision ★ VistaVision

26

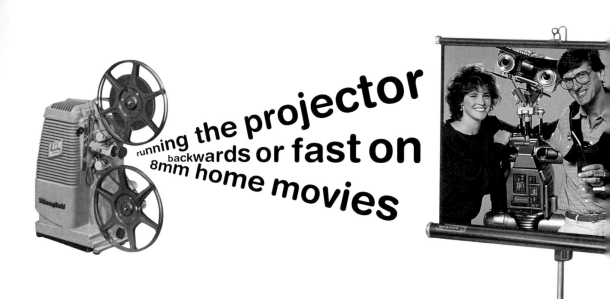

running the projector backwards or fast on 8mm home movies

"that does

not compute"

BEFORE THE MOUSE

"COMPUTERS WILL
TAKE OVER OUR JOBS"

TELEX

THE SOUND OF TELETYPE MACHINES
IN THE BACKGROUND ON NEWS RADIO STATIONS

4231600

```
0 0 0 0 0 ■ 0 ■ 0 0 0 0 0 ■ ■ 0 0 0 0 0 0 0 0 0 0 0 0 0 0 0 0 0 0 0 0 0 0 0 0 0 0 0 0 0 0 0 0 0 0 0 0 0 0 0 0 0 0 0 0 0 0 0 0 0 0 0
 1  2  3  4  5  6  7  8  9 10 11 12 13 14 15 16 17 18 19 20 21 22 23 24 25 26 27 28 29 30 31 32 33 34 35 36 37 38 39 40 41 42 43 44 45 46 47 48 49 50 51 52 53 54 55 56 57 58 59 60 61 62 63 64 65 66
■ ■ 1 1 1 1 1 ■ 1 1 1 1 ■ 1 1 1 1 1 1 1 1 1 1 1 1 1 1 1 1 1 1 1 1 1 1 1 1 1 1 1 1 1 1 1 1 1 1 1 1 1 1 1 1 1 1 1 1 1 1 1 1 1 1 1 1 1
2 2 2 2 2 2 2 2 2 2 ■ 2 2 2 2 2 2 2 2 2 2 2 2 2 2 2 2 2 2 2 2 2 2 2 2 2 2 2 2 2 2 2 2 2 2 2 2 2 2 2 2 2 2 2 2 2 2 2 2 2 2 2 2 2 2 2 2 2
3 3 3 3 ■ 3 3 3 3 3 3 ■ 3 3 3 3 3 3 3 3 3 3 3 3 3 3 3 3 3 3 3 3 3 3 3 3 3 3 3 3 3 3 3 3 3 3 3 3 3 3 3 3 3 3 3 3 3 3 3 3 3 3 3 3 3 3 3 3
4 4 4 4 4 ■ 4 4 4 ■ 4 4 4 4 4 4 ■ 4 4 4 4 4 4 4 4 4 4 4 4 4 4 4 4 4 4 4 4 4 4 4 4 4 4 4 4 4 4 4 4 4 4 4 4 4 4 4 4 4 4 4 4 4 4 4 4 4 4 4
5 5 5 ■ 5 5 5 5 5 5 5 5 5 5 5 5 5 5 5 5 5 5 5 5 5 5 5 5 5 5 5 5 5 5 5 5 5 5 5 5 5 5 5 5 5 5 5 5 5 5 5 5 5 5 5 5 5 5 5 5 5 5 5 5 5 5 5 5
6 6 6 6 6 6 6 6 6 6 6 6 6 6 ■ 6 6 6 6 6 6 6 6 6 6 6 6 6 6 6 6 6 6 6 6 6 6 6 6 6 6 6 6 6 6 6 6 6 6 6 6 6 6 6 6 6 6 6 6 6 6 6 6 6 6 6 6 6
7 7 7 7 7 7 7 7 7 7 7 7 7 7 7 7 7 7 7 7 7 7 7 7 7 7 7 7 7 7 7 7 7 7 7 7 7 7 7 7 7 7 7 7 7 7 7 7 7 7 7 7 7 7 7 7 7 7 7 7 7 7 7 7 7 7 7 7
8 8 8 8 8 8 8 8 8 8 8 8 8 8 8 8 8 8 8 8 8 8 8 8 8 8 8 8 8 8 8 8 8 8 8 8 8 8 8 8 8 8 8 8 8 8 8 8 8 8 8 8 8 8 8 8 8 8 8 8 8 8 8 8 8 8 8 8
9 9 ■ 9 9 9 9 9 9 9 9 9 9 9 9 9 9 9 9 9 9 9 9 9 9 9 9 9 9 9 9 9 9 9 9 9 9 9 9 9 9 9 9 9 9 9 9 9 9 9 9 9 9 9 9 9 9 9 9 9 9 9 9 9 9 9 9 9
 1  2  3  4  5  6  7  8  9 10 11 12 13 14 15 16 17 18 19 20 21 22 23 24 25 26 27 28 29 30 31 32 33 34 35 36 37 38 39 40 41 42 43 44 45 46 47 48 49 50 51 52 53 54 55 56 57 58 59 60 61 62 63 64 65 66
```

KELLY [5081]

TELECOPIERS KEYPUNCH OPERATORS

TICKERTAPE

MANUAL TIMECLOCKS

The Newton  Macintosh  IICi  Maccessories  Wozniak and Jobs  Apple Classic
"It's a bug, Dave."  Signatures of all developers etched into the case of the first Mac
Command Z  Graphical User Interface  NeXT  Steve Jobs' bow ties
Apple II  Localtalk  QuickTime  RISC  Moof  Elk Cloner  Festering Hate  Burp
Blackout  Rob Janov  key commands that revealed hidden images in early models

THE FIRST LAPTOPS

**All Pearl Bailey needed for a best seller was one finger and**  olivetti's studio 45: the Brightwriter

# The Palmer Method

red & black ribbons

Gregg shorthand

the smell of dittos

stenography

typing erasers

Wite-Out

microfilm

elite & pica

microfiche

dictaphones

before fax machines

learning how to type

carbon paper

typing off the paper if you didn't pay atten

photostats

PALO SOLERI'S ARCOSANTI TOMORROWLAND EXPO '67 WORLD'S FAIRS
BIOSPHERE EXPERIMENTAL PROTOTYPE COMMUNITY OF TOMORROW

A trip through space at the New York World's Fair ended on the rim of a moon crater where astronauts were exploring and experimenting.

**Space Food Sticks** thinking that Skylab would fall on your house **Fizzies** freeze dried ice cream staying up late to watch the launch Apollo, Gemini, and Mercury launches and splashdowns the Challenger disaster the Hubbell telescope golfing on the moon anti-gravity ballpoint pens **NASA** The space race

# When you're first in Color TV, there's got to be a reason.

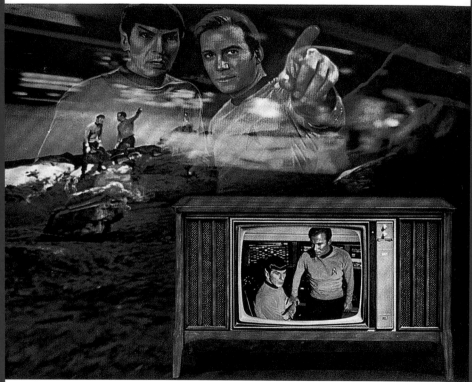

See "Star Trek" on RCA Victor Color TV. Shown above, The Hathaway

- Like Automatic Fine Tuning that gives you a perfectly fine-tuned picture every time.
- A new RCA tube with 38% brighter highlights.
- Advanced circuitry that won't go haywire.
- And over 25 years of color experience.
- You get all this and more from RCA VICTOR.

RCA

The Most Trusted Name in Electronics

38

ion propulsion rockets • transporter beams • Full body medical scanners • space

7

out of 10

[ number of engineering students
cite Star Trek as a reason
For entering the Field ]

replicators • subspace radio • tricorders • universal translators • optical transducers

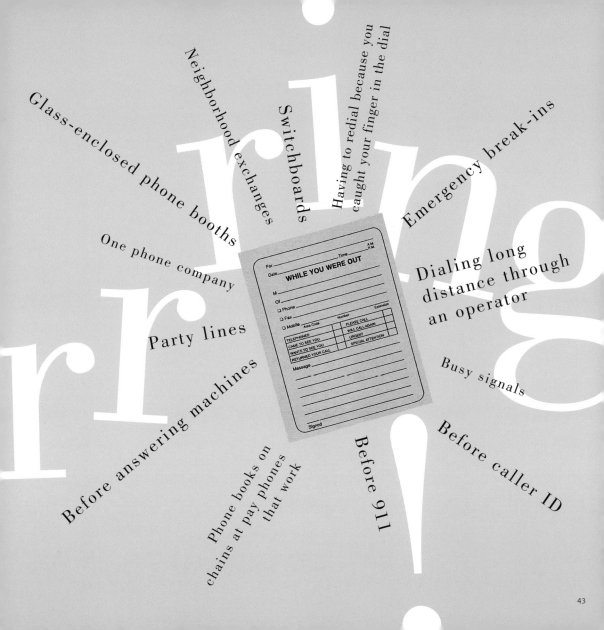

rrrring!

Neighborhood exchanges

Switchboards

Having to redial because you caught your finger in the dial

Emergency break-ins

Glass-enclosed phone booths

One phone company

Dialing long distance through an operator

WHILE YOU WERE OUT

For_____ Time_____ □ A.M. □ P.M.

Date_____

M_____

Of_____

□ Phone_____

□ Fax_____

□ Mobile  Area Code    Number    Extension

| | PLEASE CALL |
|---|---|
| TELEPHONED | WILL CALL AGAIN |
| CAME TO SEE YOU | URGENT |
| WANTS TO SEE YOU | SPECIAL ATTENTION |
| RETURNED YOUR CALL | |

Message_____

_____

_____

_____

Signed_____

Party lines

Busy signals

Before answering machines

Phone books on chains at pay phones that work

Before 911

Before caller ID

43

vinyl

tableside jukeboxes

3-inch CD singles with adaptors

close and play

Technics turntables

player pianos

car stereo

taping a quarter on the
stylus to prevent skipping

playing your first record album on
your own phonograph

hi-fi

hearing-aid style earpieces
for transistor radios

GORDON
LIGHTFOOT
Produced by
Lenny
Waronker
and Gordon
Lightfoot

THE WRECK
EDMUND FITZ
(Gordon Ligh
Moose Music Lto
℗1976 Warne
Records In
3300 Warner Blvd , Burbank

REPR

THE ERIE CANAL THE ALASKA PIPELINE **THE PANAMA CANAL THE SUEZ CANAL** THE ST. LAWRENCE SEAWAY **THE HOOVER DAM THE ASWAN DAM THE TENNESSEE VALLEY AUTHORITY** THE VERRAZANO-NARROWS BRIDGE

MACKINAC STRAITS BRIDGE

SAULT STE. MARIE, MICH.

SOO LOCKS

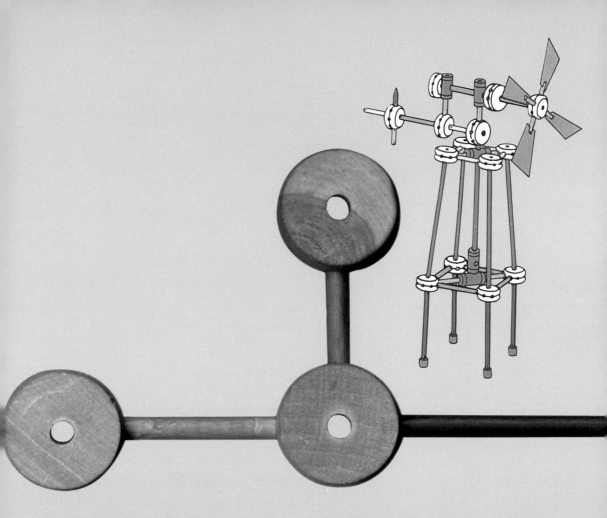

ERECTOR SETS / LEGO / LINCOLN LOGS / WOODEN BUILDING BLOCKS / HEATHKITS

Aluminum siding

# geodesic domes

Pre-fabricated homes solar power

outhouses **wind power**

hand-pump water pumps

48mb

defrosting the freezer La Machine by Moulinex
hot-air popcorn poppers *crepe*
*makers* single serving electric hamburger cookers
before Cuisinart electric frying pans
*the first Mr. Coffee* hot pots *electric woks*
hand-operated juicers Fry Daddy *fondue*
*pots* convection ovens hot dog steamers

MIRRO-MATIC
PRESSURE PAN AND CANNER
RECIPES · DIRECTIONS · TIME TABLES

MIRRO
THE FINEST ALUMINUM

*waffle irons* before
teflon metal ice cube trays with a
lever to release ice percolators
washing machines with wringers
*Washboards* carpet sweepers
foot-pedal sewing machines

relaxers

curling rods

rollers for home permanents

peroxide to bleach your hair

"Sun-In and sunlight
and you'll be blonder tonight"

hair irons

paper to roll over hair ends

sleeping in rollers

tabletop blow dryers

bonnet hairdryers
with a manicure drying fan on the motor
(belted around your waist for mobility)

electric rollers

crimpers

Jheri-Curl

dry shampoo

Dippity-Do

The

Thighmaster The rows of pulleys, that hooked over a door, made for doing leg lifts Electric saunas where your head sticks out the top, ostensibly to make you Sauna suits Sauna suits sweat, to firm up your waist, tummy, and thighs Saccharin

# Bullworker

Flex-a-lounge Joggers and track joggers Jack LaLanne workout records "Feel the burn" working out before spandex Redux

RelaxAcizor gives those "soft" abdominal muscles a real workout...while you rest!

**The No-Work Workout**

**Easy to Use**

Take It Easy!

RelaxAcizor

**Free! Mail Today!**

# POPULAR SCIENCE

MARCH · 35c *Monthly*

## CATCHING Drunk Drivers
## BEFORE THEY KILL YOU

*superhighways*

*"the door is ajar"*

*catalytic converters*

*no emissions testing*

*no fuel injection*

*t tops*

*before airbags*

*no headrests*

*three on the tree*

*Ralph Nader's "Unsafe at Any Speed"*

*Escort radar detectors*

**CAUTION TO OWNERS**

PART No. 3697081

**BREAKING-IN YOUR ENGINE**

THE CRANKCASE OF THE ENGINE IN THIS VEHICLE AS RECEIVED BY YOU IS FILLED WITH A LIGHT BODY "BREAK-ING-IN" OIL. USE THIS OIL ONLY DURING THE BREAKING-IN SCHEDULE SHOWN BELOW.

IT SHOULD NOT BE USED AFTER COMPLETION OF THE BREAKING-IN SCHEDULE-DRAIN THE CRANKCASE-WHILE HOT-AND REFILL USING THE GRADE OF OIL RECOMMEND-ED IN "ENGINE LUBRICATION AFTER 500 MILES" SHOWN IN THE CHAPTER ON "GENERAL LUBRICATION" IN THE OWNER'S MANUAL.

TO PROPERLY BREAK-IN THE MOVING PARTS OF THE ENGINE DO NOT DRIVE FASTER THAN:—

PASSENGER CARS
40 MILES PER HR. FOR THE FIRST 100 MILES
50 MILES PER HR. FOR THE NEXT 200 MILES
60 MILES PER HR. FOR THE NEXT 200 MILES
TRUCK AND COMMERCIAL
35 MILES PER HR. FOR THE FIRST 100 MILES
45 MILES PER HR. FOR THE NEXT 200 MILES
50 MILES PER HR. FOR THE NEXT 200 MILES
CONTINUOUS DRIVING AT HIGH SPEEDS SHOULD NOT BE ATTEMPTED UNTIL THE VEHICLE HAS BEEN DRIVEN 2000 MILES.

**CHEVROLET**

**DEALER: DO NOT REMOVE**

*fiberglass construction*

*gas guzzlers*

*flooding at start-up*

*white walls*

*chokes*

*no seat belts*

*fine Corinthian leather*

zone

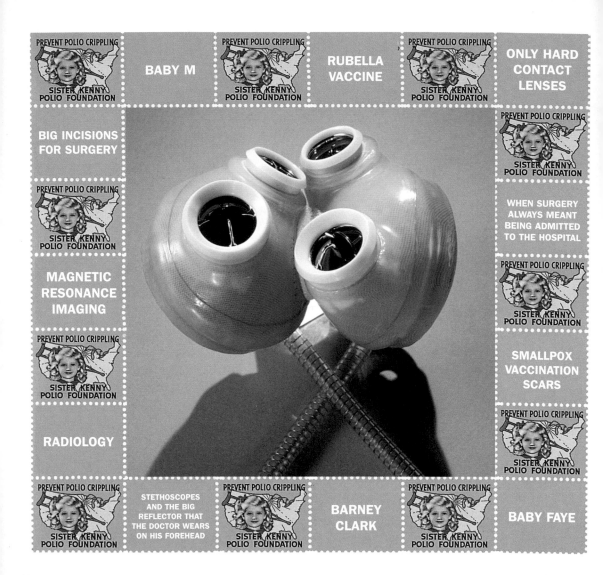

nothing to wind
...nothing
to wear out!

# *slinky*

## BY JAMES INDUSTRIES

Is it live, or is it

64 4 h b

"On January 24th, Apple Computer will introduce Macintosh. And you'll see why 1984 won't be like *1984*."

IBM ············

shake your groove thing ·············· PENTIUM PROCESSOR

Memorex?

······· WINDOWS

START ME UP

AUDIO TAPE

"RACEP Manpack is just ounces heavier than a standard telephone. The transmitter-receiver for this **highly mobile** communications system weighs **less than five pounds** and is a **compact** 2.7 x 6.2 x 6.5 inches. Manpack, with a peak power output of four Watts, will transmit **two miles** and is compatible with a larger, more powerful vehicular model."

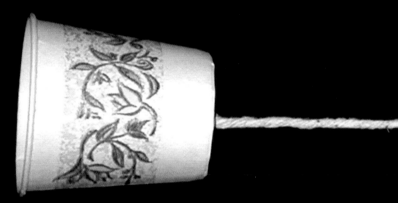

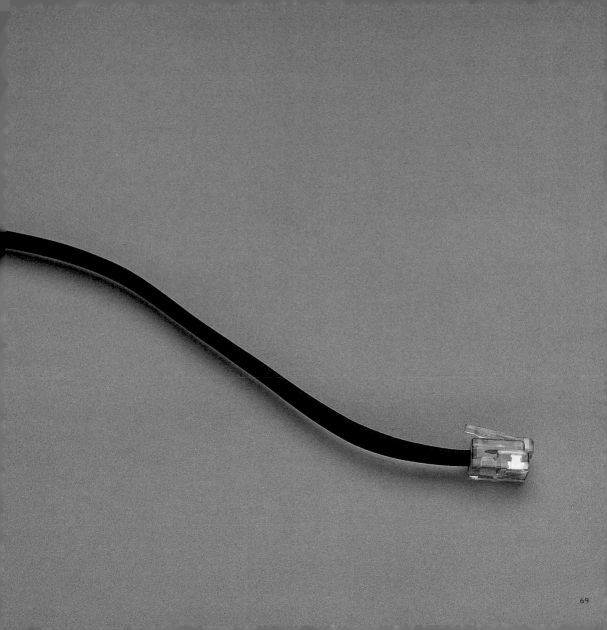

# Teletext + Videotex

# Mosaic

## 1200 baud + 14.4 modems
## Having to type in the letters

# http://

# Tim Berners-Lee

# The Source

## The fish tank site

The first time you heard "you've got mail"

## Having to learn Fortran
## or Pascal to draw a circle

Cat. No. 62-2073

Seven Dollars and
Ninety-Five Cents

# Radio Shack

# TRS-80 GRAPHICS

By J. D. Robertson and John P. Grillo

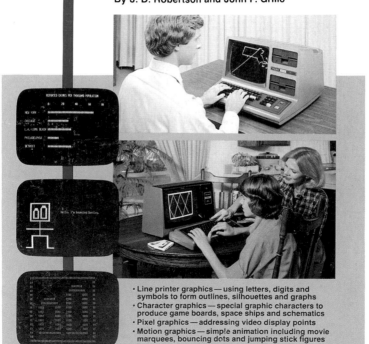

- Line printer graphics — using letters, digits and symbols to form outlines, silhouettes and graphs
- Character graphics — special graphic characters to produce game boards, space ships and schematics
- Pixel graphics — addressing video display points
- Motion graphics — simple animation including movie marquees, bouncing dots and jumping stick figures
- Sample programs · Suggested problems and solutions

# SORT + SYNC

Philip Esteridge (A)

Jack Tramiel (B)

Sheldon Adelson (C)

Ken Olson (D)

Wozniak & Jobs (E)

Mitch Kapor (F)

Adam Osborne (G)

Alan Kay (H)

Gary Tate (I)

An Wang (J)

Bill Millard (K)

Rick Inatome (L)

Philippe Kahn (M)

Nolan Bushnell (N)

Marc Andreesen (O)

Gary Kildall (P)

A 10  B 12  C 3  D 2  E 1  F 4  G 11  H 9  O 5  O 6

K 8  L 7  M 15  N 14  O 13  P 16

1 Apple
2 Digital Equipment
3 COMDEX
4 Lotus
5 AshtonTate
6 Wang
7 Inacomp Computer Centers
8 ComputerLand
9 Kaypro
10 IBM
11 Osborne
12 Atari & Commodore
13 Netscape
14 Atari
15 Borland
16 CP/M

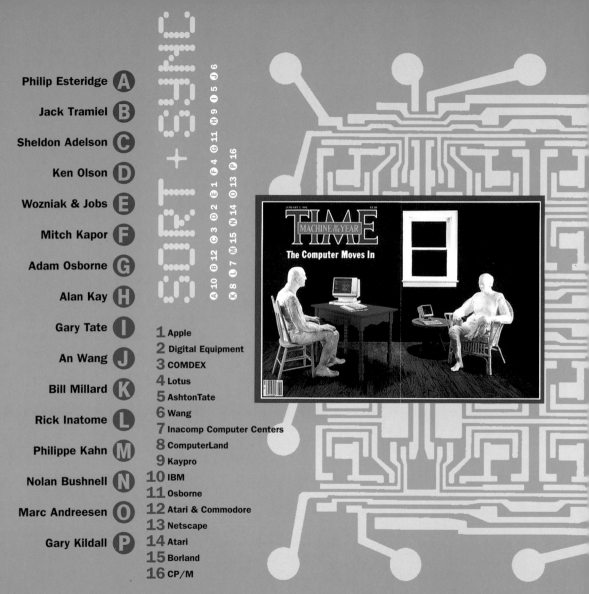

73

before direct deposit
paying bills with checks
banking before 3pm
tellers
drive-in banks    pneumatic tubes
cash

NB
D
ALPENA BANK
ALPENA, MICHIGAN

IN ACCT. WITH
DATE
12-6
12-2
:AWALS
DEPOSITS
BALANCE
ACCT. No.

THE PEOPLES STATE BANK
of ALPENA
ALPENA, MICHIGAN

SAVINGS DEPARTMENT

TAKE CARE OF THIS BOOK

If you lose or mislay it give immediate notice
to the bank.

This book must accompany all withdrawals.

See rules and regulations on last page.

register noises

protractors **compasses** long division
**the metric system** Visicalc

abacus 4-function calculators the size of a suitcase
"new" math micrometer Texas Instruments chisenbop

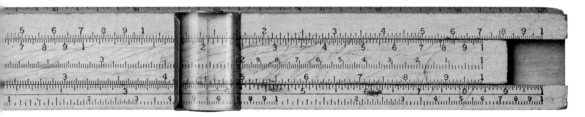

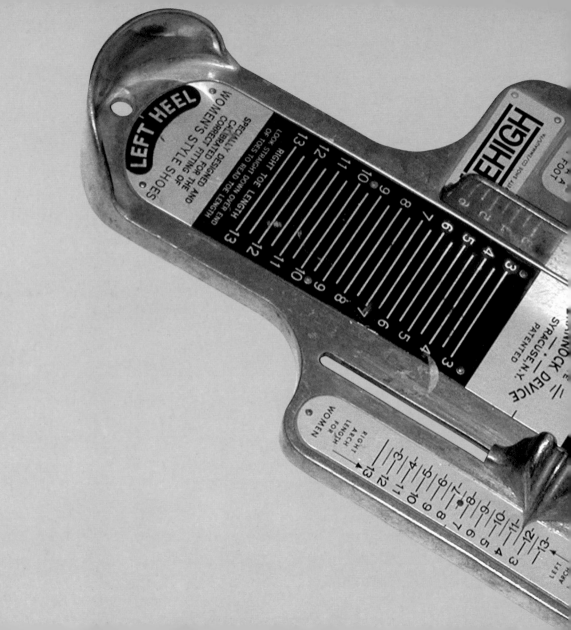

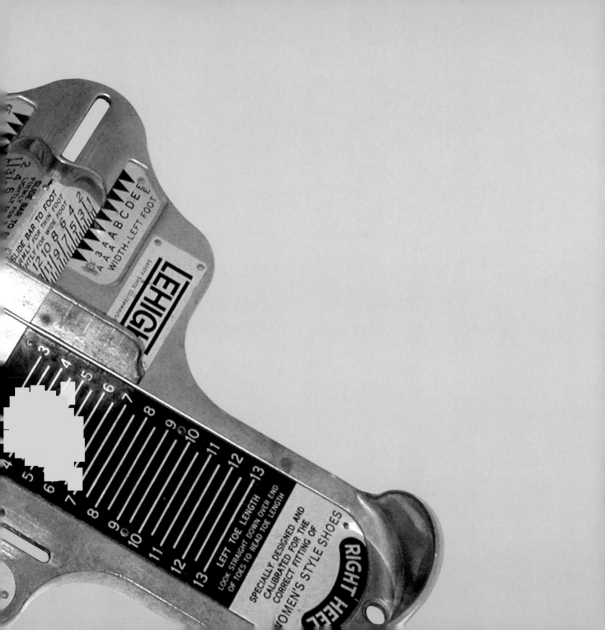

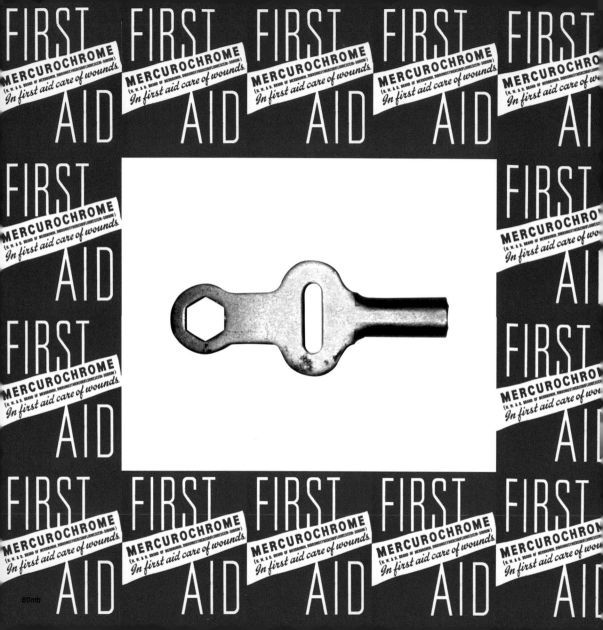

BEFORE FLUORIDE PLAQUE DISCLOSING TABLETS BEFORE NOVOCAINE
USING A STRING TO PULL A LOOSE TOOTH • MERCURY AMALGAM FILLINGS • WATER PIK
HEADGEAR • SOLID BAND BRACES • DENTAL IMPRESSIONS

LAVA LAMPS LA-Z-BOY CHAIRS VIBRATING MASSAGE CHAIRS COUGHING

ASHTRAYS ELECTRIC FIREPLACES SMOKELESS ASHTRAYS POLE LAMPS

THE PLASTIC SCREEN THAT ATTACHED TO THE TV AND MADE "PSYCHEDELIC"

DESIGNS IN SYNC WITH YOUR STEREO FIRELOGS FIBER-OPTIC LAMPS

INDOOR BARBECUE GRILLS THE CRAFTMATIC ADJUSTABLE BED

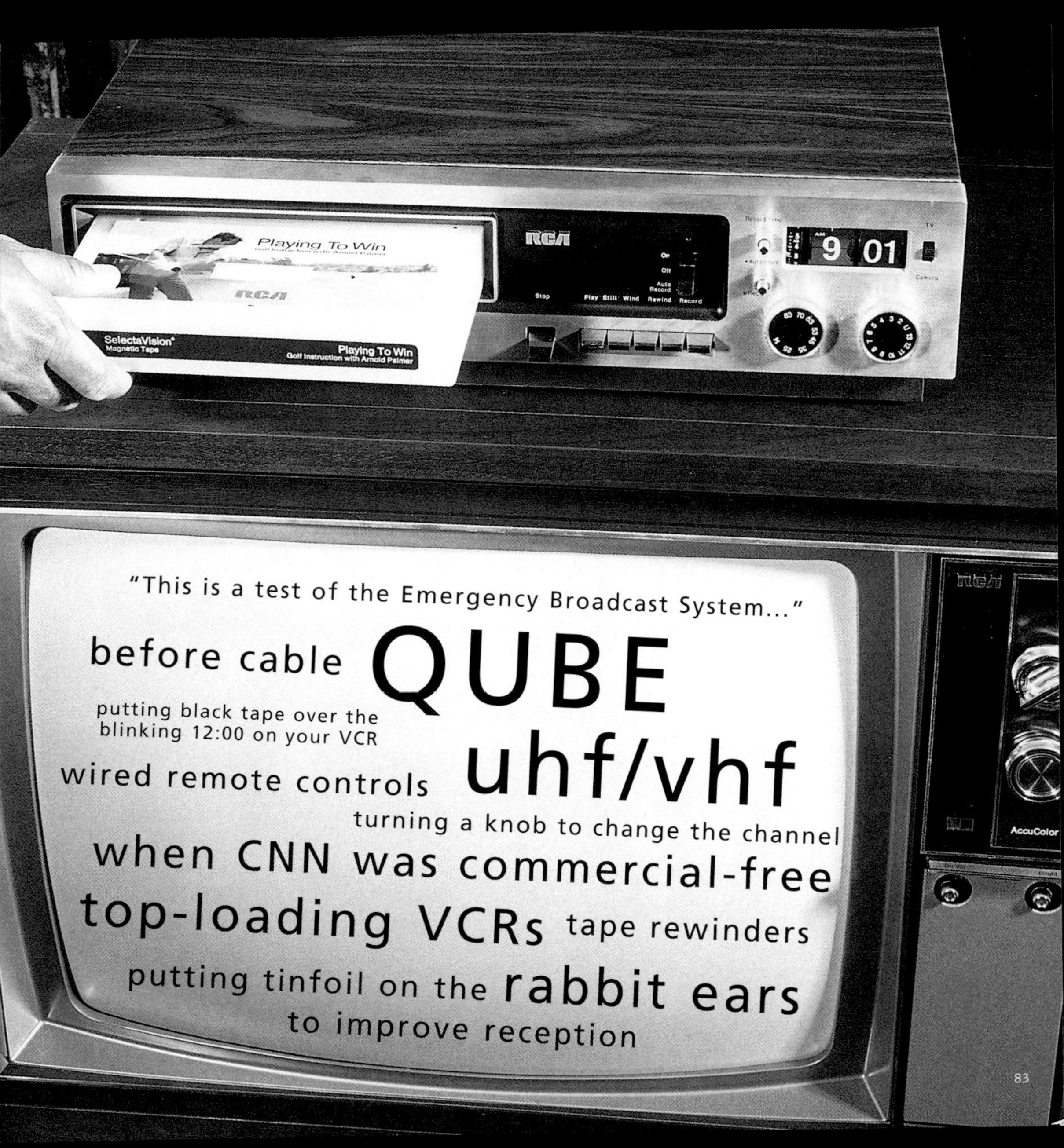

Playing To Win
RCA
SelectaVision®
Magnetic Tape
Playing To Win
Golf Instruction with Arnold Palmer
On
Off
Auto Record
Stop
Play Still Wind Rewind Record
9 01
AccuColor
"This is a test of the Emergency Broadcast System..."
before cable
QUBE
putting black tape over the blinking 12:00 on your VCR
uhf/vhf
wired remote controls
turning a knob to change the channel
when CNN was commercial-free
top-loading VCRs
tape rewinders
putting tinfoil on the rabbit ears to improve reception

weather balloons

slide projectors

black + white

Newsreels in movie theaters

# let's go to the videotape!

Doppler radar

Tex Antoine & Mr. Weatherbee

overhead projectors

photo finish

portable televisions

the watchman

Kodachrome

# BO
# BOX

**AKIO MORITA**

**THE ORANGE FOAM HEADPHONES THAT CAME WITH THE FIRST WALKMAN**

**SOUNDABOUT**

**THE RECORD PLAYERS USED IN GRADE SCHOOL WITH THE SPEAKER BUILT IN**

DRIVE-IN MOVIE THEATER SPEAKERS

KARAOKE MACHINES

O H

O F

WHEN ONLY DOCTORS HAD BEEPERS

K E

RADIOS THAT CLIPPED ON SOMETHING METAL TO RECEIVE THE SIGNAL

the SPRUCE GOOSE

BRANIFF

PAN AM

when you didn't have to
walk through a metal DETECTOR

FRONTIER

MGM GRAND

PLAYBOY JET

BRITISH AIRWAYS

sonic BOOMS

PROP planes

PeoplExpress

ill-fated DC-10s

# *Faster than a speeding bullet . . .*

*more powerful than a locomotive*

"Any sufficiently advanced technology is indistinguishable from magic."

ARTHUR C. CLARKE

LENTICULAR SCREENS
HOLOGRAMS
NUDIE GLASSES
LITMUS PAPER
3-D GLASSES
GLOW-IN-THE-DARK
SOLAR POWERED CALCULATORS
MOOD RINGS

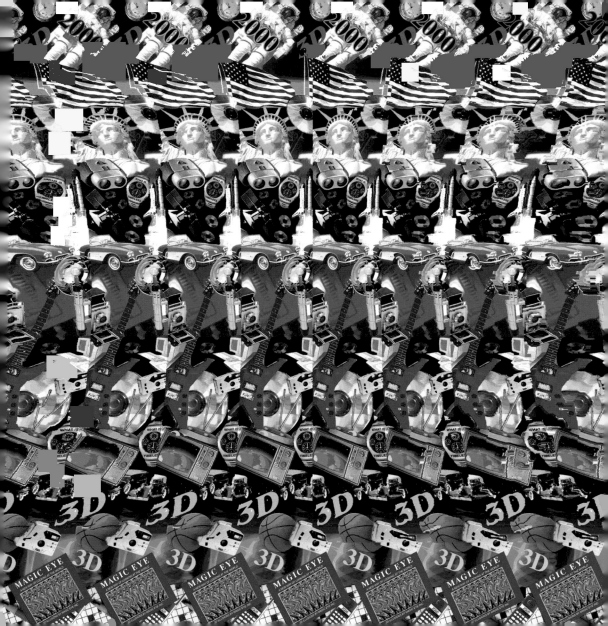

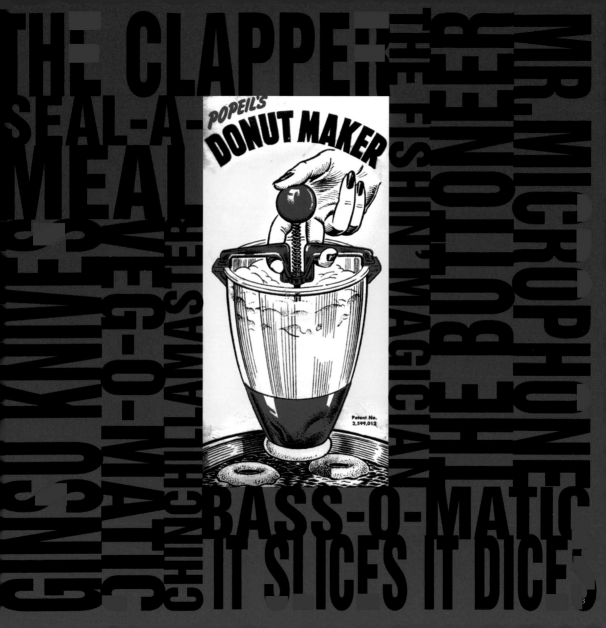

THE CLAPPER
THE SEAL-A-MEAL
GINSU KNIVES
VEG-O-MATIC
CHINCHILLAMASTER
MR. MICROPHONE
THE FISHIN' MAGICIAN
THE BUTTONEER
THE FISH'N MAGICIAN

POPEIL'S
DONUT MAKER

Patent No.
2,599,012

BASS-O-MATIC
IT SLICES IT DICES

3

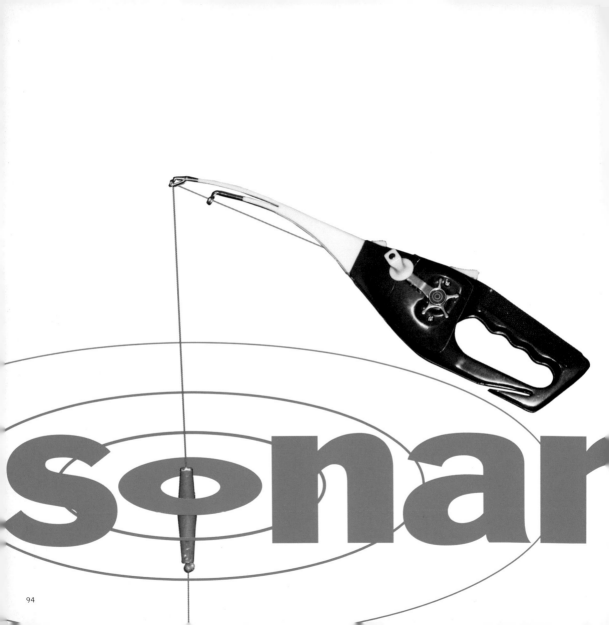

sonar

life before **microwave popcorn** the first microwaves with carousels trying to cook a whole meal in a microwave watching sparks fly the first time you put metal in the microwave browning trays urban legends of pets exploding

**PACEMAKERS**

# HOW AN AUTOMAT WORKS

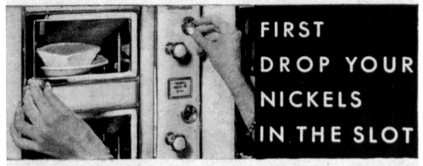

FIRST DROP YOUR NICKELS IN THE SLOT

THEN TURN THE KNOB THE GLASS DOOR CLICKS OPEN

LIFT THE DOOR AND HELP YOURSELF

*If you think it's butter, but it's not ...* Patent No.

# 111,626

to Henry Bradley for "A compound for culinary use" (1871)

AIR CONDITIONING

**a** ┄┄┄┄┄┄┄┄┄┄┄┄┄┄┄┄┄

**fiber optics**

**b** ┄┄┄┄┄┄┄┄┄┄┄┄┄┄┄┄

**xerography**

**c** ┄┄┄┄┄┄┄┄┄┄┄┄┄┄

*helicopter*

**d** ┄┄

laser

**e** ┄┄┄┄

elevator

**f** ┄┄┄┄┄┄┄┄┄┄┄┄

*medical respirator*

**g** ┄┄┄┄

**plastic**

**h** ┄┄┄┄┄┄┄┄┄┄┄┄┄┄┄┄┄┄

**TEFLON**

**i** ┄┄┄┄┄┄┄

**a** Willis Haviland Carrier   **b** Robert D. Maurer, Donald B. Keck, and Peter C. Schultz   **c** Chester F. Carlson   **d** Igor I. Sikorsky   **e** Gordon Harold Gould, Theodore Maiman, Arthur Schawlow, and Charles Hard Townes   **f** Elisha Graves Otis   **g** Forrest M. Bird   **h** Leo Hendrik Baekeland   **i** Roy J. Plunkett

the l'eggs egg • bathing caps • I can't believe it's a girdle • living bras • wonderbra • the 18-hour girdle • models in black turtle-necks modeling Playtex Cross-Your-Heart bras over their clothing in TV ads • Howard Hughes engineering a bra for Jane Russell in "The Outlaw" • lines at department stores for nylons • garter belts thigh-highs • swim suits before lycra • latch closures on galoshes

# before VELCRO

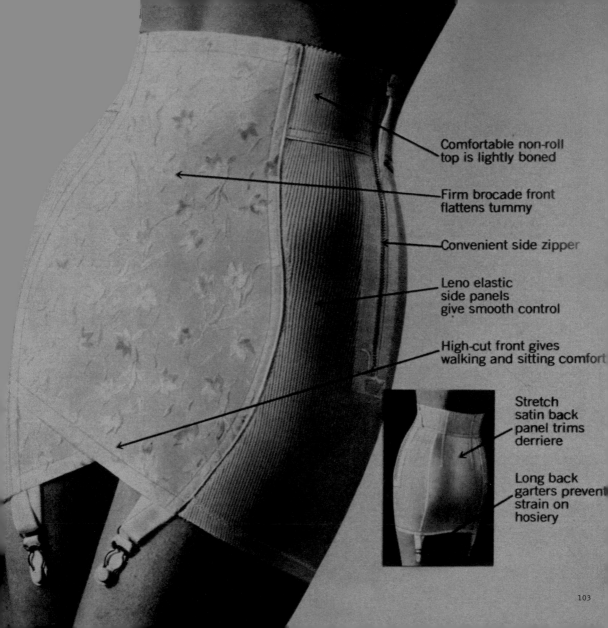

Comfortable non-roll
top is lightly boned

Firm brocade front
flattens tummy

Convenient side zipper

Leno elastic
side panels
give smooth control

High-cut front gives
walking and sitting comfort

Stretch
satin back
panel trims
derriere

Long back
garters prevent
strain on
hosiery

103

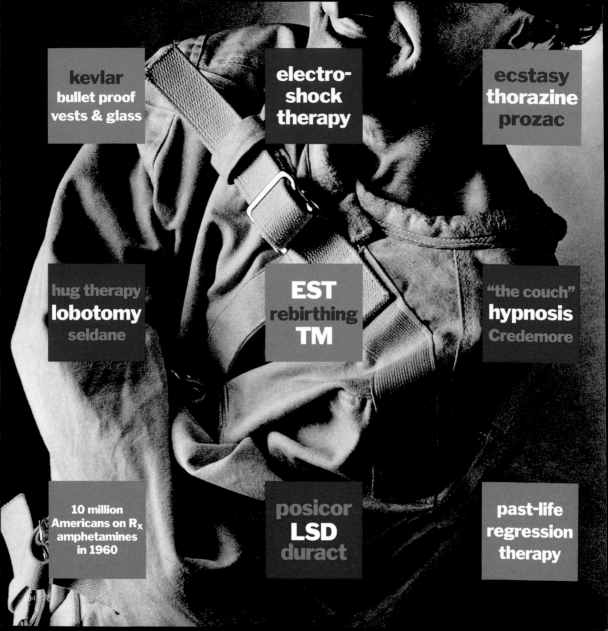

**"HIT ME WITH YOUR LASER BEAM"**

Dr. H. C. Rothenberg of GE to show "Laser Ranger" to science students

laser guns
laser surgery
the laser show at the hayden planetarium
laser tag
laser pointers
laser printers

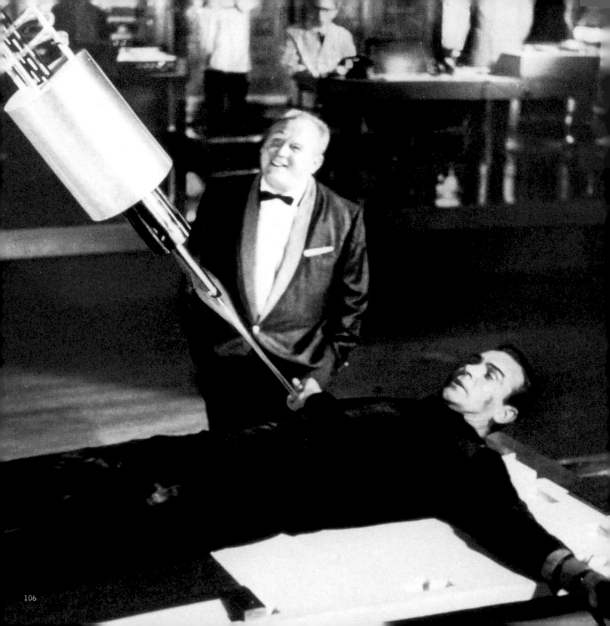

**ATTACHÉ CASE** with 50 Gold Sovreigns, 40 rounds of ammunition, infrared telescopic sight, AR-7 folding stock survival rifle, and a can of tear gas designed to look like talcum powder. **Cigarette Rocket** ignited by lighting the cigarette—a fuse embedded in the tobacco triggers the rocket out of the lit end. **CELL PHONE** controller for BMW 750il. Microcameras placed in the front of the car beam back images to a miniature television display on the cell phone. The combination of pressing 3, Recall, Send will cause a bolt of electricity to jump from the phone. It also comes equipped with a fingerprint scanner. Other features found in the BMW 750il are also controlled by the phone, such as reinflating tires, wire cutters, and missile launchers. **Whistle-activated Key Chain** emits a stun gas when "God Save the Queen" is whistled. A wolf whistle activates a highly charged explosive compound. **ACID PEN Grenade Pen PICK PEN Peton Belt DETONATOR WATCH Garrote Watch LASER WATCH Magnetic Watch PRINTER/RECEIVER WATCH** contains a shortwave receiver, paper punch, paper, and a RAM microchip which stores the message received. **Radar Watch ROTARY SAW WATCH Television Watch** contains a 1-inch liquid crystal television monitor that displays live images from any remote camera beaming a signal into it. **AVRAM LIGHTWEIGHT TRACER** that can be placed on someone else or swallowed in the form of a pill. Range is 3 miles and broadcasts for 3 hours upon activation. **Davey Tracer ECHO TRACER X Ray Safecracker** disguised as either a pocket calculator or cigarette case. A plate swings out to form a viewing screen similar to a fluoroscope. A burst battery with an extremely short shelf life generates the needed electricity to operate the safecracker.

LED **LIGHT EMITTING DIODE** LCD **LIQUID CRYSTAL DISPLAY**

SCUBA **SELF CONTAINED UNDERWATER BREATHING APPARATUS** SOS

**SAVE OUR SOULS** SST **SUPERSONIC TRANSPORT** RADAR

**RADIO DETECTION AND RANGE** VELCRO **VELOUR / CROCHET** HAL

**HEURISTICALLY PROGRAMMED ALGORITHMIC COMPUTER** WYSIWYG **WHAT YOU**

**SEE IS WHAT YOU GET** BASIC **BEGINNER'S ALL-PURPOSE SYMBOLIC INSTRUCTION**

**CODE** SQL **STRUCTURED ENGLISH QUERY LANGUAGE** SCUD **SUBSONIC CRUISE**

**UNARMED DECOY** Q-DOS **QUICK AND DIRTY DISK OPERATING SYSTEM**

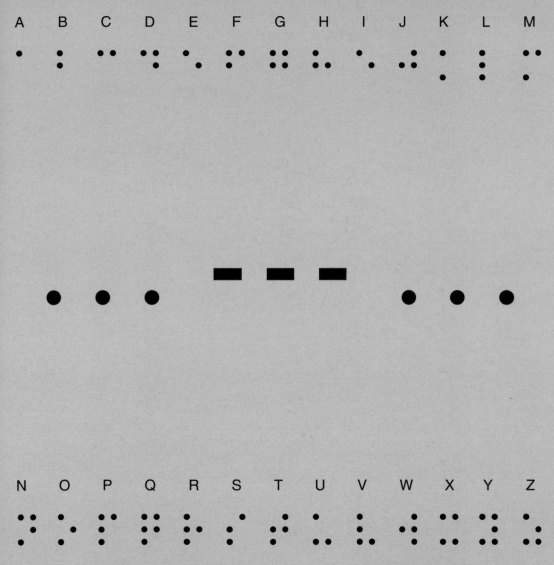

# 10

waiting for radios & 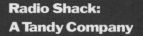 televisions to warm up

**dead air**

Radio Shack:
A Tandy Company

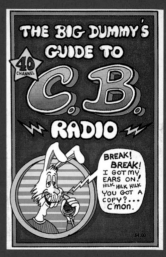

**signing off with the national anthem**

what's your handle? and 20?

**HeathKit**

**short wave**

**walkie-talkies**

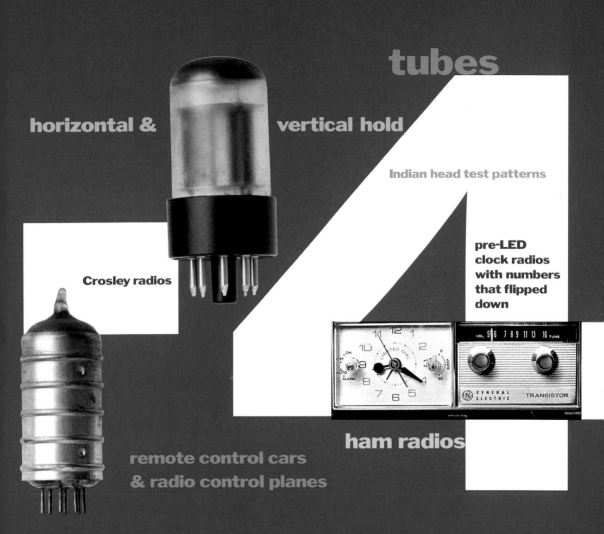

**horizontal &** **vertical hold**

**tubes**

**Indian head test patterns**

**Crosley radios**

**pre-LED
clock radios
with numbers
that flipped
down**

**ham radios**

**remote control cars
& radio control planes**

**changing channels with pliers when the knob broke**

# I need it im

## 1950 1960 1970

FIRST CLASS MAIL • AIRMAIL SPECIAL DELIVERY • TELEGRAM • MAILGRAM

## 7daysnex

> **"Our Age of Anxiety is, in great part, the result of trying to do today's jobs with yesterday's tools."**
>
> MARSHALL McLUHAN

# mediately!

## 1980  1990  2000

*TELEX • FEDERAL EXPRESS • ZAP MAIL • FACSIMILE • E-MAIL • PDF • ISDN • T1*

tdaynow

# Moore's Law (Gordon Moore, 1965)

states that memory chip performance will double every 18 months. In 26 years the number of transistors on a chip has increased more than 3,200 times, from 2,300 on the Intel 4004 in 1971 to 7.5 million on the Pentium® II processor.

# 2x every 18mo.

## com/WealthClock

**Pause, Break, Scroll Lock, Print Screen, and SysRq** • Function keys for DOS and stickers and overlays for your keyboard to help you remember them • **autoexec.bat** • config.sys • **parking hard drives** • before "ergonomic" • Homebrew Computer Club • **Syquests** • The sound of old disk drives • Elephant disks • Lotus 123 • Omni magazine • Multimate • paper for **dot matrix** printers • Bernouli boxes • 64k of RAM • double density disk drives • The **system saver fan** that fit on the sides of the Apple II to cool it down • **Curts** • Computerise Keyboard Caddy • Network Computers • Micro D • Rod Canion • Satellite Software International • **Nicholas Negroponte** • Amiga Computers • First Software Distribution • BusinessLand • Computer Factory • Crazy Eddie • Xerox Parc • Gary Kindall • Tim Patterson • Eagle Computer • Vaporware • the moth origin of the term **"debugging"** • 15-inch disks "cakeplatters" • paper tape • binary code • **Commodore 64** • Brother word processors • **8088**, the first PC-based processor • **daisy wheel** printers • b&w monitors • **gas plasma** portable computer display screens

phone

THREE MILE ISLAND
OBSERVATION CENTER

CLOSED TODAY

SOYLENT GREEN IS PEOPLE!  CONE OF SILENCE

CHERNOBYL

SNEAKERS

FLUBBER

LOGAN'S RUN

DICK TRACY'S WATCH

WILLY WONKA

CHITTY CHITTY BANG BANG

WARGAMES

DR. WHO

BUCK ROGERS  ORGASMATRON  WESTWORLD

*before shock resistant + waterproof*

**pulsar watches** quartz movements

atomic clock THE FiRST SWATCH

chronographs RADIUM TO MAKE THE NUMBERS

GLOW IN THE DARK *forgetting to wind*

*your watch* multiple time-zone displays

*"Takes a licking and keeps on ticking..."*

**stopwatches** *before second-hands*

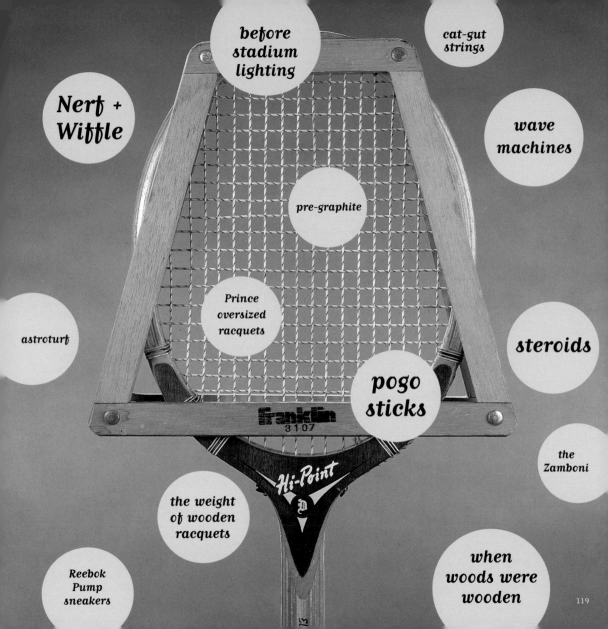

before stadium lighting

cat-gut strings

Nerf + Wiffle

wave machines

pre-graphite

astroturf

Prince oversized racquets

steroids

pogo sticks

the Zamboni

the weight of wooden racquets

Reebok Pump sneakers

when woods were wooden

franklin 3107

Hi-Point

119

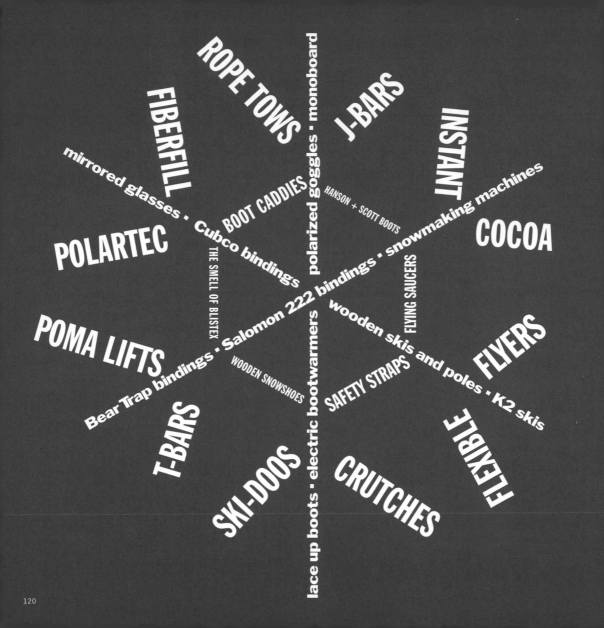

ROPE TOWS · monoboard · J-BARS

FIBERFILL · INSTANT

mirrored glasses · Cubco bindings

BOOT CADDIES

polarized goggles

HANSON + SCOTT BOOTS

COCOA

POLARTEC

THE SMELL OF BLISTEX

snowmaking machines

FLYING SAUCERS

POMA LIFTS

Salomon 222 bindings · wooden skis and poles · K2 skis

Bear Trap bindings

electric bootwarmers

FLYERS

WOODEN SNOWSHOES

SAFETY STRAPS

FLEXIBLE

T-BARS

SKI-DOOS

lace up boots

CRUTCHES

**Atari 2600** • Action Pak • Adventure • Alien • Alpha Beam With Ernie • Artillery Duel/Ghost Manor • Assault by Bomb • Asteroids • Atari Cube • Atari Video Cube • Bachelor Party • **the first Nintendo** • Bachelor Party/Gigolo & Burning Desire/Bachelorette Party • Bank Heist • Beany Bopper • Beat 'Em and Eat 'Em • Berenstain Bears • Berzerk • Big Bird's Egg Catch • Blackjack • BMX Airmaster • Boing! • Breakout • Buck Rogers: Planet of Zoom • Bump ___ mp • Cakewalk • Cave In • Changes • Chase the Chuckwagon • Chopper Command • Circus Atari • Combat • Comma ___ ndor Attack • Cosmic Swarm • Crazy Climber • Crypts of Chaos • **pinball machines** • Custer's R ___ ath Trap • Defender • Demolition Herby • Demon Attack • Disaster • Dodge 'Em • Donald Duck's Speedboat • Donkey ___ zzard • Dumbo's Flying Circus • The Earth Dies Screaming • Edtris 2600 • Eli's Ladder • Entombed • Espial • E.T. The Ext ___ Exocet • The Fall Guy by 20th Century Fox • Fast Eddie • Flash Gordon • Flesh Gordon • Frenzy • **Intellivision** • F ___ ial • Frogger II: Threedeep! • Front Line • Galaxian • A Game of Concentration • Ghostbusters • Galactic Tactic • Glib • Gr ___ emlins • **"You sunk my battleship!".** Guardian • Gyruss • Halloween • Harbor Escape • H.E.R.O • ___ Incredible Hulk • Intuition • I Want My Mommy • James Bond 007 • Jawbreaker • Journey Escape • Joust • Jungler • Kaboom! ___ ng Kong • Kool-Aid Man • Kung Fu Master • Lochjaw • London Blitz • Looping • The Lord of the Rings • MagiCard • Malaga ___ arauder • Marine Wars • M*A*S*H • Meltdown • Millipede • Miner 2049er • Missile Command • Mission Omega • ___ • Moonsweeper • Motorodeo • Night Driver • Obelix • **Mattel handheld football** • Off Your ___ kie • Omega Race • Outlaw • Pac-Man • Party Mix • Pengo • Pepper II • Philly Flasher/Cathouse Blues • Piece O' Cake • Pitfa ___ • Polaris • Pong • Pooyan • Popeye • Porky's • Q*Bert's Qubes • Quadrun • Rabbit Transit • Ram It • Rampage • Revenge of th ___ **Space Invaders table-style game** RealSports Basketball • Rescue Terra I • River Patrol • Rocky ___ mp • Room of Doom • Rubik's Cube • Rush Hour • SAC Alert • **air hockey** • Scramble • Scraper Caper • Sector Alpha ___ • Shuttle Orbiter • Revenge of the Jedi—Game II • **Merlin** • Sinistar • Sir Lancelot • Sky Lancer • Smurfette's Birthda ___ Day • Snoopy And The Red Baron • Sorcerer's Apprentice • Sound X • Space Canyon • Spacechase • Space Invad ___ Hunter • Star Fox • Stargate • Stargunner • Star Trek: The Motion Picture • Star Wars: Ew ___ Musical Match-Ups • Stell-A-Sketch • Stunt Man • Submarine Command ___ Up • Survival Island • Survival Run • Sword of Saros • Swordquest ___ Targ • Tax Avoiders • **going to the arcade** • Tempest ___ ilot • Tomarc the Barbarian • Tooth Protectors • Track & Field • Tron Deadly D ___ e • Video Reflex • Vortex • Wall Ball • Wall Defender • Warlords • Wild Western • W ___ ar's Revenge • Z-Tack • **Gameboy.** Bounty Bob Strikes Back • Cloak & Dagger • Gren ___ Shootout • Krull • **Simon** • Locomotion • Meteorites • Montezuma's Revenge • Mr. Do's Castle • Rescue on Fractalus • Space Dungeon • Space Shuttle • Stargate • Star Wars: The Arcade Game • Star Wars ROTJ: Death Star Battle • Superman III • Vanguard • Zaxxon • Zenji • Zone Ranger

wuckawuckawuckawuckawuckawuckawuckawuckawuckawuckawuckawuckawuckawuckawuckawuckawuckawucka

122

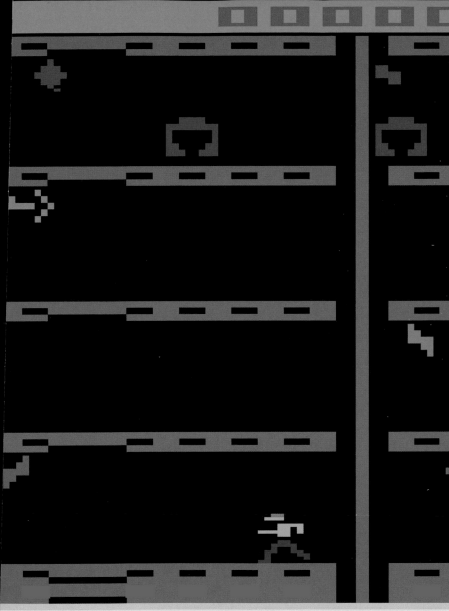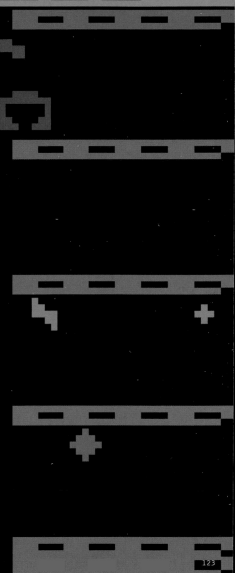

crayons ----- **a**

*silly putty* ---------- **b**

FLOWBEE ---- **c**

HULA HOOPS ------- **d**

the gas mask ---- **e**

SCOTCH TAPE --**f**

**a** Edwin Binney and Harold Smith **b** James Wright
**c** Rick Hunts **d** Richard Knerr and Arthur "Spud"
Melin **e** Garrett A. Morgan **f** Richard Drew

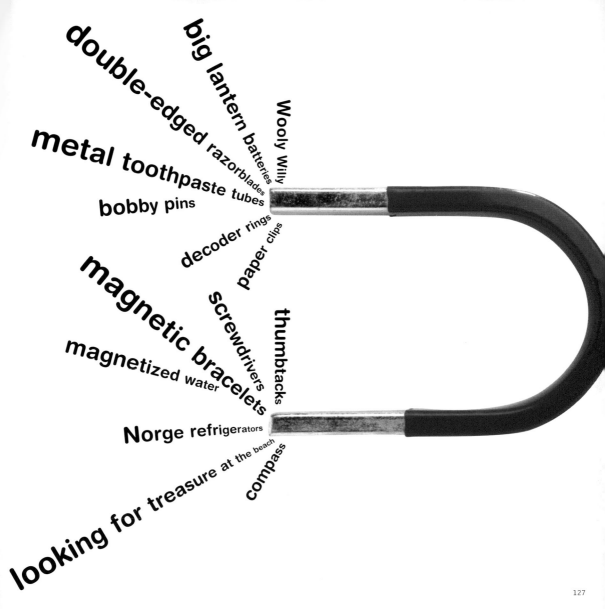

big lantern batteries

double-edged razorblades

metal toothpaste tubes

Wooly Willy

bobby pins

decoder rings

paper clips

magnetic bracelets

screwdrivers

thumbtacks

magnetized water

Norge refrigerators

looking for treasure at the beach

compass

127

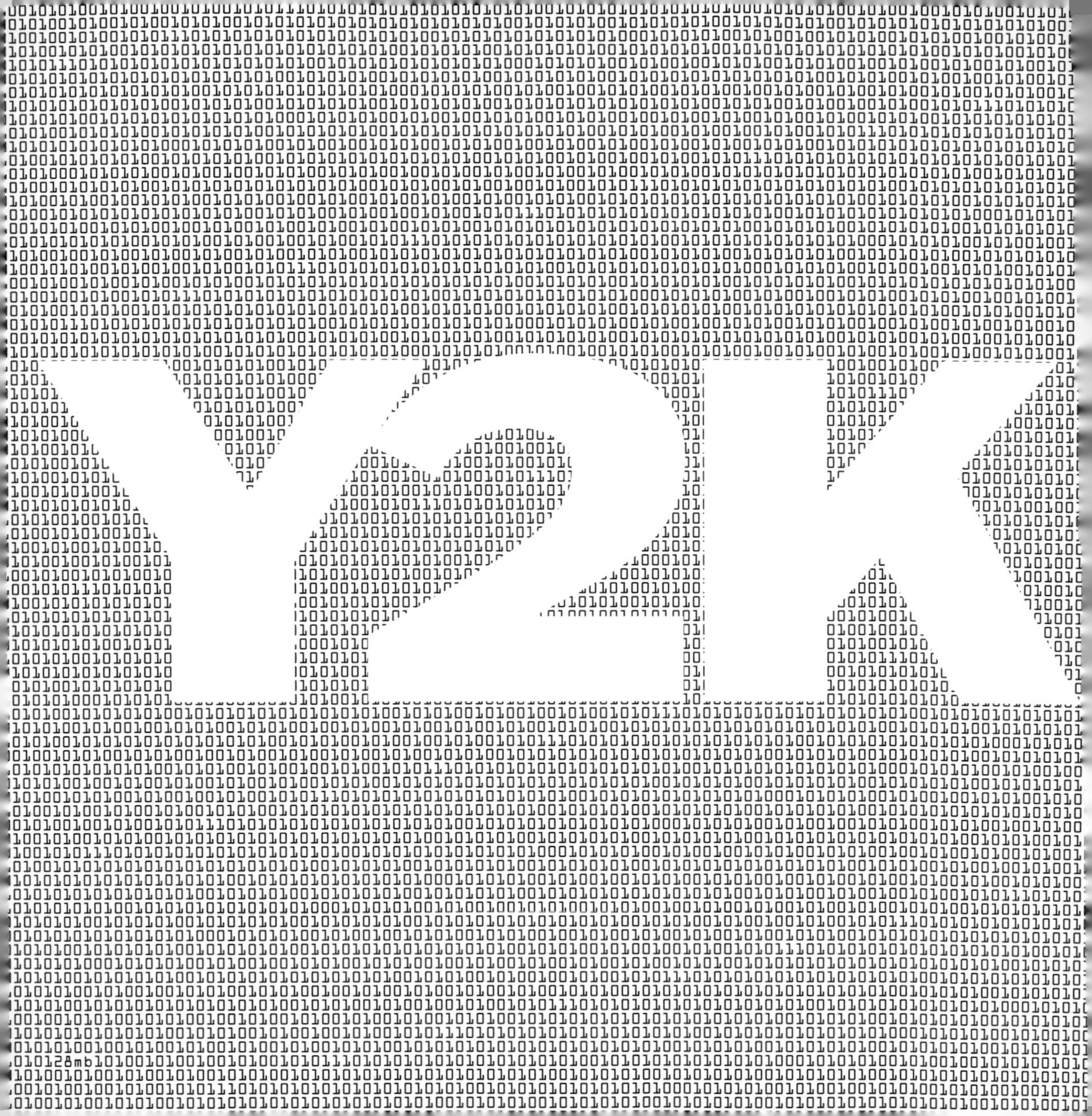
Y2K

WHAT'S GOING TO HAPPEN, DAVE?

SOMETHING WONDERFUL...

# re:

**Avery label maker** *(page 3)* As tongues tired of the lick-and-stick labels of the early 1930s, R. Stanton Avery, who came from a family of inventors, pulled paper through a cigar box of glue and developed the first self-adhesive labels. In 1935, he founded the Kum-Kleen Adhesive Products company in LA, spawning an entire industry. Avery Dennison is now a billion dollar company. **Texas Instruments Calculator Slide Rule TI30** *(page 5)* No wonder baby boomers can't do longhand division. In 1967, Texas Instruments invented the handheld electronic calculator and in 1973, they released the SR-10 "slide rule" calculator retailing at $149.95. In 1982, with the TI-30 SLR, the first solar-powered slide rule calculator, math whizzes could slip their calculator into their shirt pockets and do complicated calculations just about anywhere—except in the dark.

**Sonogram** *(page 7)* In the late 1970s doctors began to use sonograms in routine pregnancy exams to ascertain normal fetal development. Sonograms are visual images created by sound. Sonograms were once the exclusive province of professional marine and audio researchers. A sonogram does not use ionizing radiation and therefore poses no danger to a developing fetus. **VW Bug** *(page 9)* Adolf Hitler was the proud owner of the original VW Beetle or "the People's Car," developed by Ferdinand Porsche in 1933. By the late '50s, the bugs were snatched up by Americans who loved the revolutionary bubble shape and cheap price. Mexico is the only country that still produces the cult classic VW bug—retailing there at $6,000. The new streamlined retro VW Beetle, also made in Mexico, costs $20,000. **AMC Gremlin** *(page 10)* The first American-made sub-compact car was born on April Fool's Day, 1970, when American Motors Corporation introduced the Gremlin SIX–Series 40. The groovy Gremlin captured the decade with its psychedelic colors.

**Leaded Gas** *(page 11)* Between 1925 and 1985, more than 7 million tons of lead were added to gas (it was an octane-enhancing additive), coinciding with a high incidence of lead poisoning of American children. The heavy metal is considered highly toxic to the environment and to humans absorb lead through inhalation. Since the early 1970s, the U.S. has mandated a phaseout in the amount of lead in gasoline. **DDT** *(page 12)* In 1939, Paul Mueller of Switzerland discovered the insecticidal properties of DDT, and, by 1955, residual spraying of homes was used worldwide to combat malaria. Biologist Rachel Carson's landmark book "Silent Spring" (1962) revealed insects' resistance to pesticides and DDT's harmful effects on the environment and its infiltration into the food chain. In

1970, the EPA cancelled almost all uses of DDT. New research has shown that DDT can damage the developing brain. It is still used overseas. **Mouse Trap Game** *(page 13)* In 1963, Milton Bradley introduced the Mouse Trap Game where the goal is to

build a mouse trap and catch your opponent's rodent. **Rube Goldberg** *(page 14)* The Pulitzer Prize winning artist Rube Goldberg (1883-1970) is best known for his mind-boggling drawings and cartoons of complicated contraptions. Mocking the advances of technology to make complex tasks simple, Goldberg's wacky inventions turned a one-step task into a comical 50-step task. His name has become synonymous with anything convoluted! **Frisbee** *(page 17)* Leave it to Yale students to inadvertently invent the Frisbee between classes. To pass the time, some 1940s Yalies took to tossing tin pie plates back and forth—which they named "Frisbees." In the '50s, Californian Walter F. Morrison developed a plastic toy disk and worked with Wham-O Company to market these "Flyin' Saucers" in 1957. By 1959, Wham-O had appropriated the name Frisbees. College students continue to expand the use of Frisbees, and Ultimate Frisbee, created in 1967 by Joel Silver, is a mainstay of campus sport. **Easy-Bake Oven** *(page 18)* Ever since Hasbro introduced the ovens in 1963, aspiring Betty Crockers have begged their parents for an Easy-Bake. Forget real food, with an Easy-Bake Oven, you can make your own bubble gum. **Flash Extender** *(page 20)* In 1963, Kodak introduced the Instamatic camera with its cartridge-loading

film. Fifty million Instamatics were produced by 1970. **Polaroid's The Swinger** *(page 21)* Capitalizing on the swinging '70s trends, Polaroid's "Swinger," released in 1972, took black-and-white wallet size photos and was cheap ($19.95) and easy to use. Polaroid's award-winning advertising campaign featured the then-unknown beauty Ali MacGraw grooving to the Swinger jingle beat—in a bikini. Her career, and Polaroid, took off. **Qiana shirts** *(page 22)* In 1930 "Doc" Wallace Carothers invented nylon in the laboratories of E. I. duPont de Nemours & Co. Nylon was the first synthetic fiber, a predecessor of Banlon, Orlon, Qiana, and Neoprene. The invention of the superpolymer changed fashion and its manufacture forever. The *New York Times* wrote a front-page story to announce this dramatic innovation. Headlines proclaimed "Chemist Produces Synthetic Silk." ***Saturday Night Fever* 8-Track** *(page 23)* The nylon shell-encased continuous-loop audiotape systems known as "8-Track" were popular from the mid-1960s until the mid-1980s. In 1966 all Fords offered a factory installed in-dash 8-track players; in 1967 GM and Chrysler followed suit. 8-Track was the invention of William Powell Lear, who also invented the LearJet. The best-selling movie soundtrack of all-time, *Saturday Night Fever* (1977) brought together many of the pop-culture innovations of the period. **Panasonic 8-Track Player** *(page 24)* a.k.a. the "Dynamite" or "Plunger," Panasonic's

Portable RQ-830s of the early 1970s, let disco freaks really PUMP IT UP. Without an automatic track changer, you had to

hit that plunger. Sound was mono and there was no headphone jack. But you could take it anywhere. **Robot Toys** *(page 28)* As the power of the TV image solidified in the 1960s, toy manufacturers got to work.

Toy battery-operated robots modeled after the robot in the classic 1960s TV show "Lost in Space" flew off the shelves. During the Stars Wars "Trilogy Years" (1977-1983), promotional figures of the heroic droids became some of the most popular retail items at Toys "R" Us. **Punch Card from Mainframe computer** *(page 29)* From its invention as a means of tabulating the 1890 census to its widespread use in businesses, billing, and education throughout the 1940s, '50s, and '60s, the punch card came to represent computerization and the information age. Man became a number and information to be processed. Going against the words "Do not fold, spindle, or mutilate," Berkeley students in the '60s protested the "System" by burning their punch cards. But to little avail; though the punch card is now obsolete, the mentality behind it has reached unimaginable heights. **Mainframe Computer** *(page 30)* Long before the laptop, massive Mainframe computers (also called a host or CPU) dominated the computer industry. Frontrunner IBM released the IBM System/360 mainframes in 1964. A few years later, the whole world was

introduced to a terrifying futuristic mainframe brain: HAL of Stanley Kubrick's *2001*. **Apple Lisa computer** *(page 31)* Begun in 1979 and released in 1983, the

revolutionary Apple Lisa 1 was the first computer to use a Graphical User Interface. One of the masterminds behind the Lisa, Steve Jobs (he co-founded Apple computers) worked on the computer for over 3 years, driving the price up to $9,995. Legend has it the computer was named after one of Job's children. The Lisa featured a 12-inch black-and-white screen, 1 megabyte of memory, two floppy drives named Twiggy (they were reed thin like the famous model), and the very first Mouse and Trashcan. After a year and a half, Apple discontinued the Lisa and brought out the Macintosh. **Olivetti typewriter** *(page 32)* By the late 1960s, electric typewriters had superseded the timeworn manual typewriter. The Italian Olivetti typewriters led the pack, taking over their American competitor Underwood in 1959. **IBM Selectric** *(page 34)* Master inventor Alvin Snaper, director of Power Technology, developed the IBM Selectric Type Ball in the 1960s. The fast-moving metal Type Ball ended the curse of jamming keys on electric typewriters. The Daisy Wheel came next. **Epcot Center—Spaceship Earth** *(page 35)* The gigantic futuristic silver

sphere that is the Spaceship Earth at Florida's Epcot Center opened in 1982. It was hailed as the first large-scale geodesic spherical

structure and is 18 stories high, 164 feet in diameter with an interior space of 2,200,000 cubic feet. Inside, visitors can take a diorama-filled time-travel ride through the history of communication—from Cro-Magnon cave art to the Information Age, space technology, and beyond. It's no surprise that Science Fiction writer Ray Bradbury helped create it. **Tang** (page 37) The powdered juice mix, Tang, short for tangy but sounds like tangerine, was introduced by General Foods in 1959. Alvin Snaper was the inventor. In 1965, Tang accompanied the astronauts on the Gemini spaceflights and all spaceflights through the Apollo 11 moon landing in 1969, establishing Tang as a futuristic food. **Skylab** (page 37) America's first experimental space station, Skylab, was launched on May 14, 1973, from the NASA Space Center. Teams of three manned the Skylab workshop for 171 days and 13 hours. The unmanned Skylab made its planned return into earth's orbit on July 11, 1979, scattering debris over the Indian Ocean and calming fears that pieces of Skylab might fall out of the sky. **RCA Color Television** (page 38) The couch potato wasn't far off when, in 1954, RCA began production of the first commercial color television set—first with a 15-inch picture tube and later that year, a 21-inch screen. Dwight D. Eisenhower was the first President to be broadcast in color in 1955. **Motorola Star Tac phone** (page 39) Phasers on. The high-tech Motorola Star Tac series is the smallest and lightest cellular phone on the market. Plus, the futuristic flip-cover lets you feel just like Captain Kirk. **Panasonic R-72 "Toot-a-Loop"**

(page 41) Developed around 1970, the Panasonic "Toot-a-Loop" was an AM radio designed to be wrapped around the wrist. To accessorize your bold new fashion statement, stickers were supplied. **Princess Phone** (page 42) Introduced in 1959, the compact Princess telephones were a major design improvement on the clunky phones of the time—and the dial was located on the handset. Targeting designing women, the phone came in various colors. And what about that name!

**GE Show'N Tell** (page 44) Filmstrips were to elementary school kids in the '60s and early '70s what videos were to the '80s and websites to the '90s: a learning resource. A filmstrip, used to expose a series of slides or photographic stills, could be projected onto a screen, viewed with a handheld viewer or shown on the GE Show'N Tell. A 45-rpm record could be played in tandem with the film. **The Mackinac Bridge** (page 46), one of the world's longest suspension bridges between cable anchorages—5 miles long—opened to traffic in late 1957. The bridge, designed by engineer Dr. Davie B. Steinman, connects Michigan's Lower and Upper peninsulas. **Tinker Toys, Lincoln Logs, Erector sets, Lego** (page 47) In 1913, former Olympic medal winner (Pole Vault) A.C. Gilbert creates the Erector Set, in 1914, stonemason Charles Pajeau develops Tinker Toys, and, in 1916, John Lloyd Wright (son of Frank Lloyd) invented Lincoln Logs. The common denominator in these classic toys: kids like to build. Add plastic and color in the '60s and you've really got a hit: Lego (established in 1932). **Infra-Red Cooking** *(page 49)* Marketed in the late 1950s, infrared Cooking made roasting small game over a spit a safe, domestic option. Homemakers could watch as thermal radiation of wavelengths longer than those of visible light toasted, broiled, and baked just like an oven could. **Sunbeam appliances** *(page 51)* Appliance giant Sunbeam brought shiny chrome-plated electric kitchen gadgets to the new "sub-urban" communities that flourished after WWII.

**Max-Pax** *(page 52)* One of the earliest innovations in coffee culture was packing ground coffee in vacuum-sealed tins, which eliminated grinding coffee beans. Freeze-dried coffee and instant coffee offered a faster cup of Java and less sediment. Then came Mr. Coffee, Melitta, and Starbucks. **Supermax Dryer** *(page 53)* With the Supermax hairdryer, women could forgo their weekly wash-and-set beauty parlor trip. The Supermax was a bright orange handheld cross between a toaster and a vacuum cleaner. Hot air rushed over infrared heating coils to whisk moisture away. **Jack LaLanne** *(page 54)* In his classic jumpsuit (pre-spandex days), motivational bodybuilder Jack LaLanne worked out with lazy Americans on his popular TV show in the 1950s and '60s. All you needed was a kitchen chair. LaLanne's innovations include the first leg extension machine—not to mention those gyms. At 85, the "Godfather of Fitness" is still buff. **Sun-Lamp** *(page 60)*

George Sperti, the developer of the Sperti Tanning Systems, was in the early 1940s one of the world's authorities on "tuned" ultraviolet rays. He also developed technology that could adjust UV rays and put Vitamin D in milk. **The Jarvik Heart** *(page 62)*, developed by Dr. Robert K. Jarvik in the late 1970s, was still being used in 1985 as a bridge to organ transplantation. Barney Clark, the first Jarvik recipient, made headlines when he lived for 120 days with the artificial implant. **The Slinky** *(page 63)* is the brainchild of shipyard engineer Richard James. In 1943 while mounting a spring device for the ship's torsion meters to recoil from heavy gunfire, a coil jarred loose, "climbed" down a pile of books and became a craze for the neighborhood children. His widow, Betty James, is still the CEO of James Industries, one toy "David" that never sold to the "Goliath." **Recording device** *(page 64)* Long before rock and roll, recording devices helped save the world for democracy. During WWII, inventor Marvin Camras used wire recorders to record battle sounds, which, after being amplified by thousands of watts, were placed strategically to mislead the Germans on D-Day. **The Dixie Cup** *(page 67)*, first manufactured in 1905, is the beneficiary of one of the most successful advertising promotions in history, one that rendered the flimsy paper cup a household name. Creator Hugh Moore participated in the anti-germ campaign that helped make the 19th century's common drinking cup obsolete. **Phone cord** *(page 68)* The original phone cord was not a cord at all; it was cloth-covered induction coil, clothed to correspond to the phone's color. Later, as plastic became standard, the colors were molded in the plastic of the cover. The first phone color? Basic black, of course. **Dancing Baby** *(page 70)* Despite wide misconception, the Dancing Baby did not cha-cha into life on the Ally McBeal show. He was actually born in a lower rent district—the Internet—where he enjoyed underground sensation status. His cameo TV appearance led to accolades and stardom for inventor Unreal Pictures, Inc.

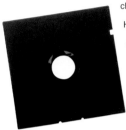

**Floppy Disk** *(page 72)* Alan Shugart made his fortune—and we do mean fortune—as the inventor of the Floppy Drive, while working for IBM in the late 1960s. It was one of his engineers, David Noble, who developed the world-changing concept of 8" flexible media inside of a cloth-lined jacket. Hence the Floppy Disk. **Bank Books** *(page 74)* The first savings pass books included both a physical description and extensive biographical information of the owner. **Cash Registers** *(page 75)* Cash registers first appeared at the inventor's popular bordello, the Pony House, a saloon and gambling emporium

in Dayton, Ohio. James (Jake) Ritty used tokens instead of coins to keep track of his revenue. The Dietzgen **Slide Rule** *(page 76)* is only one of Eugene Dietzgen's ingenious engineering products. In 1892, he invented Van Dyke paper—a translucent paper used to make an early form of white prints.

The product, which continued production into the 1960s, had no relationship whatsoever to the Dick Van Dyke Show's popularity. **Shoe Size Measurer** *(page 78)* Before the Brannock Device, shoe salesmen like Charles F. Brannock had only two options to measure feet: a crude measuring stick, or keep trying on shoes till something fit. Since receiving its patent in 1927, the company has grown very little—it employs only 14 workers—and changed very little about the late Mr. Brannock's invention. However, they are, at last report, considering a digital model. **Skate Key** *(page 80)* The first roller skates were skating wheels that attached to the shoes, developed in Germany in 1870. **Plaque disclosing tablets** *(page 81)* The Dental Plaque Tablets Crest developed in the 1970s have never gone out of style for dentists. Chewing on the tablets reveals pink-stained areas where plaque appears. A higher-tech version of the old plaque tablet is a recent addition: an ultraviolet plaque light reveals plaque after a fluorescent solution is swirled in the mouth. The **TV dinner** *(page 82)* was introduced by Swanson during WWII because cans and metals were rationed during the war. **Aluminum cans with pop tops** *(page 82)* Canned Coca Cola was first introduced in the domestic market in 1960. **VCRs** *(page 83)* became available in the late 1970s. The first iterations were gigantic by today's standards and because of the top-loading mechanism, you couldn't put your TV on top of them. They weren't cheap either. The **Concorde** (page 88) , the fist supersonic jet, made its maiden voyage in 1969. Breaking the sound barrier, the Concorde cruises at Mach 2 and can get from NY to London in 3 and a half hours. The first commercial Concorde flights (Air France and British Airways) took off in 1976. Only a handful of Concordes is in existence today—they're super expensive and make a hell of a lot of noise. **Magic Eye** (page 91) The first black and white random dot stereogram was invented by Dr. Bela Julesz in 1959, as an experiment to test patients' ability to see in 3-D. In 1991, Cheri Smith and Tom Baccei invented Magic Eye® images, igniting a worldwide stereogram explosion. By developing a patented algorithm, they were able to add color, graphics patterns and scenes to this interactive, illusionistic art. The **View-Master** (page 92) was first seen at the 1939 World's Fair. Invented by William Gruber, the View-Master 3-reel sets allowed 3-D viewing of everything from National Parks to popular TV shows and movies such as "Captain Kangaroo," "The Munsters," and more recently Jurassic Park. In 1989, Tyco Toys took over View-Master. Not just for kids, during WWII the military used the View-Master to ID airplanes and ships. **Donut Maker** (page 93) Ron Popeil, inventor of the Pocket Fisherman (page 94), the Veg-o-matic, and the Donut Maker, began as a baker at county fairs. His book, now out of print, is called The Salesman of the Century. One of his only product failures

was the Inside the Outside Window Washer. **The Microwave Oven** (page 96) was the result of a melted candy bar in the pocket of Dr. Percy Spencer, a self-taught engineer with Raytheon Corporation. He was testing a new vacuum tube called a magnetron when he discovered the melted candy. The testing of the tube on other foods left him literally with egg on his face (when a yolk exploded during early tests) but also with a patent that revolutionized the cooking industry. **The Automat** (page 98) was a fixture of popular culture for many years, appearing in everything from Edward Hopper's 1927 painting Automat, to Doris Day movies. Among the recipes cultivated by Automat "cooking"—cream cheese & olive sandwiches. **Toaster** (page 100) The first Electric Toaster appeared in 1909. It was not automatic—when the toast appeared ready, you pulled the plug. The industry was vastly improved 10 years later when Charles Strite invented the modern, timer activated, pop-up toaster. Presliced bread by Wonder in 1930 advanced technology further—consumers bought 1,200,000 toasters that year. There are no statistics as to the number of newlyweds purchasing those items. **Xerox** (page 101) is the invention that no one wanted. The first patent was applied for in 1937, and, between 1939 and 1944, inventor Chestor Carlson was turned down by more than 20 large corporations including

IBM, Kodak, and General Electric. Luckily they later reconsidered, and many trees died. **Velcro** *(page 102)* was discovered rather than invented. Swiss Mountaineer George de Mestral was frustrated by the burs that clung to his clothing. While picking them off, he realized the possibility of a fastener that would eventually overtake the zipper. It didn't quite, but it did make putting ski clothing on much much quicker. **Braille** *(page 109)* Before the invention of the Braille alphabet in the 1800s, the established method of reading and writing for the blind was embossed Roman letter. This method is still used in some schools in America. Samuel Morse did not just invent the **Morse Code** *(page 109)*. He also pursued a number of other schemes to support himself as a "serious" artist, among them the fire engine pump. The

telegraph was his most successful invention. **CB radio** *(page 110)* Al Gross, the inventor of the first "walkie-talkie" (1934–41) is considered the father of CB radios. Thanks to Gross, truck drivers can gossip and warn each other of "Smokies" on the "citizens band" along the long lonely stretches of America's highways. **Ham Radios** *(page 110)* With the advent of amateur radio kits in the late 1940s, would-be engineers could set up shop in their garages and "Ham" it up to other "Hams" (i.e., amateur radio operators). Engineer Howard Anthony invented the first Heathkits in 1947, bringing assemble-it-yourself, affordable electronics to the masses. Heathkit production ended in the mid-'80s. Who had the time? **Osborne Computer** *(page 115)* Developed by Adam Osborne in 1980, the Osborne 1 was one of the first portable computers to hit the market. It could fit under an airplane seat, weighed 24 pounds, had a 5-inch screen, and was a bargain at $1,795. Osborne Computer Corporation made its first million in 1981, but IBM and Apple were on its tail and in 1983, Osborne declared bankruptcy. Richard Sears began Sears stores moonlighting from his job as an agent of the Minneapolis and St. Louis railway station. While he usually sold lumber and coal to local residents, on one fateful day he had the opportunity to re-sell a shipment of watches at a nice profit. **Watches** *(page 118)*, he discovered, were much easier to haul than lumber, and the R.W. Sears Watch Company was established in 1886.

**Didn't find your fondest memory in Do You Remember Technology? Phone, or fax it, to us for Volume Four at (212) 873-7223. Or e-mail us your suggestions. Reach us online at TakeItBack@aol.com or at www.doyouremember.com**